True Stories

Mark Dion, Renée Green, Larry Johnson,
Karen Kilimnik, Raymond Pettibon,
Jack Pierson, Jim Shaw

Foreword

"I was meant to know the plot, but all I knew was what I saw: flash pictures in variable sequences, images with no 'meaning' beyond their temporary arrangement, not a movie but a cutting room experience."
Joan Didion, The White Album

This book celebrates the work of seven US artists who are currently emerging to international acclaim. Their work has not yet been shown in Britain. Yet its impetus corresponds with a growing impatience in the west, with both the ethos of the market and media saturated 80s; and the despairing allegories evolved by artists in response to them. This work suggests strategies for survival or simply, acceptance. Its relation to the spectator is always inclusive, inviting recognition and participation within the spaces it creates and the stories it tells.

The exhibition which this publication accompanies is presented in two stages. The first focuses on the work of Larry Johnson, Karen Kilimnik, Raymond Pettibon, Jack Pierson and Jim Shaw. They are not a group; neither are they bound by a single location, generation, aesthetic or agenda. They do share one common thread however, that is a basis in an American vernacular. Visible in all their work are its myths, master narratives, prevailing ideologies, and their inverse: fractured and irreconcilable realities and the survival strategies, pathologies or apathies of inner lives.

Part Two features Mark Dion and Renée Green, both of whom explore the interface between America and the world. For them the themes of travel, adventure, discovery and retrieval expose the darker narratives of political and environmental aggression and aggrandisement. More than that, they unpick presumptions about a dominant American culture and reveal the complex yet obscured reciprocities that exist around the process of cultural import and export. Both have chosen the institution as their model; and in their particular concern with the museum they acknowledge a debt to the work of Marcel Broodthaers. This second part therefore is presented alongside a survey of his work.

Putting together this exhibition and book from across the Atlantic has been made possible by the inestimable efforts and good will of the American Fine Arts Co., Linda Cathcart, Tom Cugliani, Feature, Jennifer Flay, Pat Hearn, Jöhnen and Schöttle, Metro Pictures, Christian Nagel and 303 Galleries. Special thanks also to Gavin Brown for all his help, Martin Cox and Gwen Darien at LACE, Los Angeles and Barbara Kruger for their kind support.

We are also grateful to the following for lending works:
Flora Biddle, New York; Gavin Brown, New York
Eileen and Michael Cohen, New York
Edward R. Downe, Jr., New York
Joyce Eliason, Los Angeles; Mike Finney, California
The Arthur and Carol Goldberg Collection, New York
Linda and Jerry Janger, Los Angeles
Mame Kennedy, New York; Jeff Kerns, California
Pablo and Leslie Lawner, California
Barbara and Howard Morse, New York
Thomas Nordanstad, New York
Eileen and Peter Norton, Santa Monica
Andrew Renton, London; Danna Ruscha, Los Angeles
Barry Sloane, Los Angeles
Judy and Stuart Spence, South Pasadena

This project could not have been realised without the generous financial support of *THE ANDY WARHOL FOUNDATION FOR THE VISUAL ARTS* and *THE HENRY MOORE SCULPTURE TRUST*.

Finally, we would like to express our thanks to the artists, many of whom have created new works specially for the publication and the show, both of which stand as a tribute to their energy and commitment.

Iwona Blazwick and *Emma Dexter*
Curators

True Stories

What follows are some chapter headings which attempt to plot recent developments in American art. Though the featured artists are disparate in age, origin and methodology, they are bound by their relation to the social, to the vernacular and to that mid ground between the subjective and the objective and between fact and fiction.

An American Landscape

As River Phoenix ejaculates, in the film, *My Own Private Idaho*, a vision appears to him of the Little House on the Prairie, l990s style. The abiding American dream has become a peeling bungalow which crashes from mid air onto a scrubby piece of wasteland. But it's home. The landscapes evoked by the artists in *True Stories* are similarly tarnished, either garbage-strewn and toxic; or patently fake, cinematic set design or ersatz historic. These topographics describe the cities in which these artists now live and work - New York and Los Angeles - but also their origins, ranging from New Bedford, Massachusetts to Tuscon, Arizona. Like David Byrne's eponymous film, their work is embedded within a vernacular which is quintessentially American. It is subject therefore to the mythologising effects of 20th century mass media.

Jack Pierson presents a flanuerish reworking of the road movie ethic and brings it to a meandering halt. Narratives of mobility, escape or discovery are dismantled with laconic apathy. He loiters at petrol stations, rests up at seedy hotels and wanders along the decrepit boulevards of once glamourous resorts or dilapidated suburbs. This is the promised land, now tainted, scattered with the carcasses of dying industries and no-go public housing projects. It's portrayal by Pierson appears unfocussed, mesmeric.

His over exposed images and snapshot framing gives this landscape the resonance of an unconscious place, intuitively imaged in the mind's eye. Neither vicarious tourist nor earnest documentarist, Pierson photographs himself, and his friends, 'beatniks without a beat'[1] as immersed in their surroundings, equally debased yet obdurate. This imagery embraces what appears as a wasteland and reveals it as just a place where people live. The landscape is redeemed through the eye of memory; unlike 'the superficial inducements of the exotic' experienced by Walter Benjamin's 'foreigner', they are enriched by the 'deeper motives' of 'travelling into the past' not, 'looking into the distance'[2].

African American artist Renée Green travels a different terrain her role as diasporic investigator[3] neatly mimicking that of the explorer/anthropologist. She evokes the Northeast of America through her quotation of its architectural style. "I'm interested in a New England version of the narration of the United States... clapboard houses, hidden and locked rooms..."[4]. Here lies the geographic location for the mythic 'birth' of a nation, the point of arrival for the British. From Worcester to Boston, Massachusetts is named almost entirely after British counties, towns and even villages - when the English arrived they called it 'vacuum domicilium'. The authority and resonance of its architecture rests on associations of good breeding, propriety and austerity. The domestic buildings of the founding families have been converted into civic institutions such as colleges, or museums. History is thereby monopolised by a single genealogy, which "...can be expanded to include that of a nation, the United States... What characteristics form a nation and culture? What sorts of stories are told about the nation, and which stories are left out?"[5].

The graphic vision of Walt Disney and Hanna-Barbera present another American panorama, networked around the globe. The acidic pastorals of the animated cartoon are 2 dimensional yet perspectively boundless. Larry Johnson deploys their glorious reductivism and claustrophobically interlocking forms in his *Winter Landscapes*. Like Bing Crosby's *White Christmas* their rampant artificiality and snowbound climate paradoxically locates them as Californian; (and in a way reminiscent of Richard Hamilton's seminal painting, Johnson also reworks his scenes in negative). Another reference to the original behind this scewed picturesque is the incidence of billboards, which rear up along every freeway. Set in a vivid and dreamy winterland Johnson's elliptical monologues disturb the silence, their parade of linguistic genres enunciating the noir morphology of the sunshine state.

Dear Reader

All the artists in this exhibition have a specific yet differing relation to narrative. In the case of Dion and Green, the meta-narratives of colonialism, discovery, taxonomy and naturalism are deconstructed. Both Pettibon and Johnson approach the vexed question of autobiographical revelation: "There is no writing which does not devise some means of protection, to protect against itself, against the writing by which the 'subject' is himself threatened as he lets himself be written: as he exposes himself" [6]. Pettibon acknowledges the existence of a contract between reader and writer of confidence and honesty (heightened by his intimate handwritten texts); a contract which he strives to undermine by presenting myriad voices, creating a "democracy of split personalities" [7].

Johnson presents a series of disembodied voices that hover within a Disneyesque landscape that has become coldly inhospitable. Suggestive of desocialization, he presents a world of competing and alienated egos "a chorus of public voices dealing with one private hell" [8]. By affecting the tone of the Problem Page or Astrological Guide, he seduces the reader/viewer into expectations of honesty and revelation which are smashed through a combination of brevity, absurdity and camp. Johnson admits that he is not interested in the emotions themselves but in the form or tone of delivery: the confession, the relief and gush of self explanation or justification. The voice of melodramatic exasperation and self deprecation is essentially camp, confiding yet distant and mask-like, acting as a perfect allegory for Johnson's textual infidelities. By referring to the process of writing within the work, both artists tempt the reader to believe in a flimsy autobiographical truth, as in Johnson's "During the late hours, when my syntax starts to run into brick walls..." or Pettibon's confession: "An unhappy writer am I", but elsewhere disabuse the reader, as in Pettibon's "So occasional, so accidental, so full of the echoes of voices that are not his - not the artist's, not the artist's muse, nor

even the voice of the man himself - that he is not to be trusted."

Using the visual language of the comic in which narrative unfolds in multiple frames, Johnson and Pettibon focus upon the single frame; potentially a fragment of a larger work, they leave space for the viewer/reader to provide the previous and subsequent story. Both make a virtue of compression, cramming a big story into a small space, propelling and curtailing the narrative drive at the same time; in fact their work is "about stories" [9]. Pettibon's work draws on a stock of American imagery ranging from railroads and baseball, to hippies and drug culture; it combines fragments of unspecified l9th century literature or idioms with present-day vernacular phrases, all delivered in the same elegant yet idiosyncratic graphic style. Its effect is to present multiple voices and myriad experiences. "My drawings are drawn from so many points of view that have literally thousands of personalities" [10]. With the simplest and oldest of materials, brush, ink and paper, Pettibon conjures work that is genuinely existential: a recurring image of a diminutive hooded figure bellows into a wilderness of snow and ice : 'Vavoom!'

Jim Shaw's *My Mirage* consists of some 170 elements arranged in 5 chapters, episodic yet separate. Shaw has devised a history of Billy, an adolescent who, assaulted by the temptations of the secular and consumer world, experiments with sex, drugs, rock and roll, and eventually with a Manson style clan. Shaw conflates the undercurrents of US vernacular culture with high art influences: psychedelic album covers, comics, Mad Magazine, Peanuts, Dr. Seuss, High School Yearbooks, Blake, Magritte, Dali, Rauschenberg, Kline. Shaw also acknowledges the influence of William Burroughs employing jarring shifts of style and narrative. There is no clear chain of events, only scattered clues amongst an assault of the senses. A vast array of contemporary signs and symbols culled from the specious and arcane intermarriage of rock music and evangelical religion are reflected in an equally eclectic array of media including gouache, pencil, oil, stained glass, records, videos. Shaw has nevertheless held to rigorous formal and temporal restraints: always employing a 14" x 17" format, these are the dimensions in which the artist absorbed second-hand art in his hometown library. Billy's psychological development over time is charted by changing visual styles appropriate to the period. Shaw takes the viewer on a pilgrim's progress through the undergrowth of post-war American culture as Billy searches for some 'vestigial spirituality through symbols drawn largely from the spiritually bereft arena of American vernacular culture' [11].

Karen Kilimnik's scatter assemblages are engaged in the fictions wrought by TV, film and reportage, 'found events', recreating actual events at third hand. Her influences range from *The Avengers* and *King of Comedy,* to incidents that have been colonized by media exploitation, for example the mass schoolyard killing that was immortalized by the Boomtown Rats' *I don't like Mondays* or the Manson Family murders. Other scenarios hint at unhappy childhood memories, and the wish fulfilment fantasies of the adolescent.

Renée Green's use of narrative and vernacular is of an entirely different order. She adopts an analytical approach to popular culture, using film and literature as tools in their own deconstruction. By presenting examples of film history to accompany exhibitions she reveals the encoded messages of mastery and cultural prejudice which formed popular conceptions of Africa in the West. A subtitle in a 1930s movie made by 'explorers' Osa and Martin Johnson, says, 'With gun and camera they go into deepest, darkest Africa'. Green also draws upon key texts from Black literature such as Richard Wright's *Native Son* or Harriet Jacobs' autobiographical *Incidents in the Life of a Slave Girl*; she places them alongside privileged authors such as Melville or Hawthorne, presenting as simultaneous their diverse accounts of history.

Fans

Jim Shaw documents the teenager's search for some meaning to life in the absence of traditional rites of passage or community control. The figure of the adolescent is a pervasive motif also appearing in the work of Pierson, Pettibon and Kilimnik. Carlyle spoke of a national disease of Adolescence. In our own times, it can be viewed as a state of mind rather than a physical process. This shift results from changing cultural and social restraints - the moment of adolescence can be extended or curtailed according to circumstance. The figure of the teenager stands as a metaphor for a moment of oblivion, of anti-authoritarianism, sexual discovery,

susceptibility, creativity, belief, naiveté. It can be celebrated or sought as a time before the burdens of work, family, property become paramount. Jack Pierson creates an aesthetic of 'hanging out', of living for the day to day mundanities, getting by on little money, celebrating the simple virtues of friendship and reinvesting sex with romance. By contrast Kilimnik's adolescent aesthetic is one of isolation and neurosis: redolent of the lonely teenager locked in her room, she indulges in lurid and often violent fantasies of power and revenge in the face of an unattainable and uncaring world of glamour. Her *Jane Creep* drawings, enact with minimal means, the revenge fantasies of the victim for the schoolyard bully. In both Kilimnik and Shaw, not only is the subject matter adolescent, focussing upon heroes and inadequacy, but so is its realisation. Kilimnik finds weak and pathetic materials, junk and trivia, disposing them in a disordered fashion, generating the effect of 'a jelly-fish timidity', 'a self effacing shrinking violet with a case of stage fright' [12]. Shaw mirrors the obsessiveness of adolescence in his collage of minutely detailed pencil drawings, records and videos, baseball cards, 'slinkies', plastic monsters and cabalistic signs and symbols. The work of Raymond Pettibon has associations with youth culture: in the past he has provided the graphic design for album covers, and has attempted to define a hippy aesthetic within his work, to express a dislocation of the senses achieved through the use of psychedelic drugs. Pettibon's hippies are the mindless surfers of Venice Beach, their political views based on conspiracy theories, their rebelliousness a pose, their commitment, to self oblivion.

Symptomatic of adolescence is the persona of the Fan: obsessions with celebrities, the search for heroes and creation of anti-heroes. Pettibon regularly uses the figure of the baseball player as an icon of all American manhood; while on the other hand he shares with Shaw, Kilimnik and Johnson a fascination with Charles Manson and 'the family'. Manson's activities have now entered American mythology alongside events such as the assassination of President Kennedy or the death of Marilyn Monroe. Incorporated into Californian history, the Manson saga simultaneously conflates the apparently immortal mythologies of celebrity, glamour, rock and roll, drugs and religion, with murder, racism, pathology and the threat of political upheaval. It is a socio-political microcosm of the tensions still in play within American society. Shaw parodies it in his parallel reconstruction of the history of the times, with a Manson style cult leader whose chief claim to fame is the ritual slaying of a dog. In a recent work *Mrs Peel....We're Needed* 1992, Kilimnik has collapsed the gory evidence and props found at the site of the Sharon Tate murders with camp paraphernalia from *The Avengers,* stranding rescue attempts within a paralysed and fantastic realm. Johnson's work *Untitled, Classically Tragic Story* obliquely references the Tate murders as distilled by time and reportage, and by narrating the events he fictionalizes them. Set within the dream factory of Hollywood the murders have been absorbed and rationalized as a movie plot, with ironic twists and turns of fate.

Kilimnik's alter ego fan possesses all the attributes of the psychopath, willing to destroy the object of adoration in an act of infantile symbolic sacrifice. The fascination with stars and celebrities teeters on the brink of psychosis, like Rupert Pupkin (Robert De Niro) in Scorcese's *King of Comedy,* or the Sandra Bernhardt character in the same movie. Jack Pierson's drawings give voice to a persona lured by the glamour of Hollywood, where romance and envy jostle for dominance. In *Silver Jackie*, he presents a tawdry empty stage, a site for the dreams and projections of the viewer .

American Psycho

Hannibal (*Silence of the Lambs*) and Henry (*Portrait of a Serial Killer*) have become iconic figures, monsters who rear their ugly heads over the horizon of contemporary cultural predilections. Hannibal, who echoes Manson, is larger than life, charismatic, inviolable, messianic - he kills to satisfy his unappeasable appetite. Henry on the other hand is a non-person, mind-numbingly ordinary, a character without psychology or motive. He kills at random and with dispassion; it is an activity which reminds him that he is alive. The third element in this bizarre conflation of fact and fiction is the spectator/ participator, most chillingly depicted in Tim Hunter's *River's Edge*. Based on a true story the film shows the naked corpse of a high school kid strangled, for no apparent reason, by her boyfriend; and goes on to examine the response of their school friends. It is one of apathetic curiosity. To the disbelief of their old rocker friend and their radical hippy teacher, they feel and do nothing.

The figure of the psychopath and the activity of serial killing present some compelling formal and symbolic possibilities. The former can be seen as the flip side of a redemptive god. He is indestructible, all seeing; he presents a belief system and demands of his followers the obliteration of self. Therein lies his power, as articulated both by Jim Shaw's cult leader in *Esse* (see plate section); and by Pettibon in his dark portraits of messianic 'visionaries'. He stands as the mirror opposite of transcendence, and indeed the reverse of the utopian dynamic of modernism. Critic Ralph Rugoff has further suggested that this figure is also of interest to artists because he occupies a position they once held: shamanistic and unassimilable, outside the boundaries of legality, rationality and the bourgeoisie; in short they are motivated by nostalgia. The indistinguishable killer however, holds a different potency. His or her ordinariness and possible infantilism - the psychopath has the epistemological range of a 10 year old - is hinted at in Kilimnik's installations and Jane character. She evokes a grungey bedroom full of weird mementos, and fetishes. Its insane occupant creates anxiety precisely because of his or her innocence. Like Richard Prince's 'Jokes' paintings, or Bruce Nauman's clowns, the patina of a smile hides a lurking malevolence or profound social disorder. Cady Noland has commented in her textual sculpture, *Towards a Metalanguage of Evil*: 'the psychopath shares the societally sanctioned characteristics of the entrepreneurial male. Their maneuvers are differentiated mostly by decibel, the acts of the psychopath being the 'louder'.' This killer has become the symptom of a pathological society in thrall to capital. Indeed, the dehumanised, 'off the shelf' multiplication of the event of killing presents an ironic reworking of the process of mass production; whilst the appeal of seriality is stimulated by that literary invention on which pop culture depends - the cliff-hanger. Finally the scene of the crime presents a grotesque installation in its own right. Again, Kilimnik exploits the ritualised mark-making and arrangements of both corpse and environment so graphically described in reports of the Manson killings: arcane graffiti daubed in blood; clothing, weapons and victims' smashed possessions in chaotic trails, as if left by a bored and messy child.

The Purple Rose of Cairo

The artists of *True Stories* create a space of participation, a zone which combines the artificial neutrality of the gallery and the 'real' events of the outside world, oscillating between site specificity and non-site. In this they echo the theatre of minimalism; the world of consumption imaged by Pop Art; the linguistic, deconstructive and archival strategies of conceptual art; and the fragmentation inherent in Arte Povera.

Beyond this arena, comes the prevalent influence of film, television, comics, but here again the work displays a wide variety of strategies for dealing with 'immersion in the world of appearances' [13]. By creating a fantasy film set Dion invites the viewer to become a participant, like Mia Farrow stepping into the action on screen in *The Purple Rose of Cairo*. Dion examines contemporary attitudes to science and technology through their cinematic archetype, Dr. Frankenstein, father of genetic engineering. Taking the flicker of the silver screen he gives it substance, presenting its fiction as a real experience. Similarly Kilimnik invites the viewer to walk through scenes from a favourite TV show, movie or song. Scattering narcotics across the floor and daubing red paint on the walls she leaves evidence of a *Suicide by Overdose and Enormous Blood Loss*. She is not concerned with either symbolism or mimesis. This installation is in a truly Brechtian sense, both representation and actuality.

Pierson too, affects the strategy of the film or TV set, setting up false walls and domestic mise-en-scène, yet he has no fiction to restage. Denying the urge to introduce new forms into a world already crowded with objects, he presents real things - tattered, worn and stained - that attest to lived experience. The site of glamour has been specifically replaced with the everyday.

Survival

'Through historical conventionalisation, have the notions and strategies of institutional critique perpetuated the fiction of art as socially transformative, or replaced that fiction with the necessary paradoxical bind of critical complicity/ complicit criticality?' Joshua Decter [14].
The political and social response to the emergence of the AIDS virus has ignited anger and action amongst the art and gay communities of the United States. Wary however of ideological entrenchment some groups have rejected classic strategies of agitprop. Instead they adopt and *détourn* the very terms of abuse and otherness they have been assaulted with (vis groups such as 'Queer Corps' or even 'Infected Faggots', themselves off-shoots of 'Queer Nation'). They adopt a pragmatic and investigative approach towards those omnipresent yet suppressed taboos of American society: pornography, sex and death. The hidden agendas of the body beautiful or of the media propagandised nation-state are simply ignored. Filmmakers such as Richard Linklater or writers Dennis Cooper and Douglas Coupland are only two of a number of practitioners who have identified a new subject, 'a subject without a mission, a fate, or even a subjectivity (at least in the superadequate Modern sense), the slacker inhabits an atomised universe: everyone speaks a debased or hybrid argot, worships at their own jerry-built altar, proselytizes for a private religion. Master narratives do not, in short, adhere... the slacker is doomed to wander an affectless void, unredeemed. Anarchy percolates in this dysfunctional landscape but never exceeds a slow boil; conspiracy theories abound, yet authority remains simultaneously monolithic and curiously beside the point' [15]. Acknowledging the influence of artists such as Larry Clark and Nan Goldin, or film maker Van Sant, Pierson marks out a laisser-faire survival strategy by increments. The casual, diaristic aesthetic signified by the snapshot - a feature of all their work - establishes a reciprocity between subject and artist, an intimacy which is part of an everyday continuum. Invisible, repressed or outlawed states of being, ranging from taking drugs, through adolescent sexuality to the messy business of dying, are returned from the orbits of exoticism into the ambit of daily life. Terms of derision are recouped, as in Pierson's, *A Fag, a Crip and a Chick: Three Lives on the Rocks* where 2 men, one in a wheel chair and a woman stand enjoying a day at the sea. The use of camp can provide a space of liberation, as Johnson has commented "One of the ways I would like to see my works functioning as 'of interest to gays' is as camp. Camp is an area in which I can claim ownership."

Artists ingest, or immerse themselves in the mass imaginary of commodity culture presenting their subjective, bodily experience of it rather than maintaining a critical distance or an attitude of apocalyptic futility. Kilimnik's approach to the society of spectacle is to utterly submerge herself in it, overlaying one screenplay, stage set, celebrity persona or music track on top of the other. This implosion of fantasies defunctionalises them, setting off bizarre and unexpected conjunctions and meanings on the verge of spinning out of control. The consistent thread of violence, massacre or suicide that runs thematically through her choice of scenarios becomes camp through the sheer staginess of her installations, equal parts scatter gun and strategic design. If the avid consumption of these projections and narratives can be likened to doing drugs, then what immerses the viewer is their effect: 'Drugs, it turns out, are not so much about seeking an exterior, transcendental dimension - a fourth or fifth dimension - rather, they explore fractal interiorities.' [16] The viewer enters the world of the solipsist, the space of one survivor, its walls covered with posters of Madonna and *Backdraft*.

Other artists penetrate institutional networks like a virus, adopting their methodologies, rituals and structures, 'complicitly critical'. Dion and Green have variously metamorphosed into reporter, curator, critic, scientist, academic, explorer, detective, publisher, film-maker. They have transported whole systems of data gathering into galleries. These artists strategically redefine their roles as intermediaries between the artworld and other cultural, scientific and political constituencies.

They dare to enter restricted zones: 'The best thing about being an artist is that you don't have to constantly ask for someone's permission...' (MD) They are specialists who dismantle the hierarchies of specialisation. They are travellers for whom the world is not a tabula rasa to be owned and named; but whose gaze attempts to see that which has been made invisible. They have become compilers of definitions and specimens to expose the collector's agenda of empire. No presumption is left unturned, no orthodoxy unchallenged. The key to this strategy lies however in reciprocity, not counter dogmatism.

Dion sets up partnerships with other practitioners and offers his services to anthropologists, zoologists or geographers in an effort to transform through co-operation. Green invites the writings and thoughts of others into her creative space taking the viewer with her on a journey of revelation. She explores the dynamics of import and export, of the complex

reciprocities between north and south inextricably bound up in language and culture yet traditionally obscured. Neither present finite works; both artists have continued the making of an installation on site throughout the course of an exhibition. Stressing non-linearity, their open-ended, non-hierarchical methodology exposes the ideological constrictions of a site; and admits gallery or institutional staff and spectators as co-workers.

Embedded in the psychological dramas of contemporary America this work does more than hold a mirror to its surface. It exposes its fallacies whilst holding onto the realities of the here and now; and suggests strategies for dismantling master narratives, with 'true' stories .

Iwona Blazwick and *Emma Dexter*

[1] Jack Bankowsky, 'Slackers', *Artforum,* November, 1991
[2] John C. Welshman quoting Walter Benjamin, 'City of Quartz review' *Art & Text,* 1992
[3] 'Being a diasporic subject myself, I have no linear history' Renée Green, interview with Donna Harkavy, 'Bequest' catalogue, Worcester Art Museum, Massachusetts, 1991
[4] ibid.
[5] ibid.
[6] Jacques Derrida, 'Freud and the Scene of Writing', quoted by Terry R. Myers, 'Hard Copy', *Arts* Magazine, Summer, 1991
[7] Michelle Plochere, 'A Conversation with Raymond Pettibon', *Artweek,* Feb., 1992
[8] Larry Johnson interview with David Rimanelli, *Flash Art,* Nov / Dec, 1990
[9] Byron Coley, 'Dreams Not Sprung from the Bush of Madonna', *Forced Exposure,* Winter, 1988
[10] ibid.
[11] Lawrence Rinder, 'Jim Shaw', *Matrix,* Berkeley University Art Museum, 1990
[12] Jerry Saltz, 'The Kid Who Never Cleaned Her Room', *Galeries* Magazine, July, 1991
[13] Dick Hebdige, 'Swimming Underwater: The Concept', Imagination Building Catalogue, 1990
[14] Joshua Decter,'Decoding the Museum', *Flash Art,* Nov / Dec, 1990
[15] Jack Bankowsky, 'Slackers', *Artforum,* November 1991
[16] Avital Ronell, Crack Wars: Literature Addiction Mania, University of Nebraska Press, 1991

Mark Dion

'The tropical rainforest ecosystem is often seen either as a lost paradise (paradise before the fall) or a green hell, a site of vast hidden wealth, or an incomprehensible treasure trove of diversity. These kinds of Romantic ideas, the most prevalent being notions of fertile paradise or the jungle as the progenitor of evil, are all western visions that inform contemporary reporting and decision making about the fate of the rainforest...

As an artist, my expertise is the field of represent-ation, and it's very clear to me from sampling the discourse around the tropical deforestation issues that there's a lot of work to be done in that area. It is particularly important for conservation organisations and the scientific community because they tend not to be very good in dealing with complicated issues of the politics of representation...

The system of taxonomy was really necessitated by the museum, which is an extension of curiosity cabinets and natural collections of the 16th and 17th centuries. Within this practice, it is necessary to have a complex system of classification and description of natural objects, in terms of science...

The explorer and the naturalist make sense of the dangerous and mysterious world around them through the process of naming, destroying some of the otherness and the exotic-ness. By putting everything into an international, supposedly objective schema, through this task (which is Adam's task) of naming the animals, naming the plants, and naming geography, man compensates for his inability to understand the natural world. The naturalist and the explorer make sense out of chaotic otherness by containing it in an established framework...

Playing with the fascination surrounding the personality of the naturalist is another extremely interesting element of the project. The naturalist in the 19th century embodies a whole bunch of dichotomies, intentions and relations that aren't really found in other characters. For example, this character obviously has a kind of machismo, but the machismo is about orchids and collecting butterflies. He is involved with science and classif- ication, but at a psychotic and obsessive level. The person who is at the forefront of colonial exploration is at the same time the first to argue for conservation. The character who is logical, rational and systematic also does not have common sense and completely disregards personal safety and comfort...

The tactical element of what I do in terms of a strategy in art production is to use fictional characters to discuss "real" material situations and documentary practice. When I wanted to talk about biological technologies as I did in a previous project recently, I used the fictional characters of Victor Frankenstein and Clark Kent to ask some very concrete questions...

The representation of nature has always been a fundamental subject in art. The very category of nature as we know it is going through so many drastic changes. The theory of evolution was a major paradigm shift in the way we considered nature. Since then nature has gone from being something we had to be protected from, to something we have to protect. We're now going through another shift brought on through biological technologies and genetic engineering. We're now producers rather than simply consumers...

Extinction changes the rules of what taxonomy does. It's no longer an enumeration of what exists in the world, but what is disappearing. There is obviously a correlation between the colonialist's endeavour to name the animals as they are discovered (Linnaeus' project) and the conservationist's endeavour to name the animals as they disappear (the endangered species list). Most of our ecological problems can be traced directly back to colonial interference. My work may not be grass roots conservation, but it is very much allied with political and ecological movements. I think it can be helpful to them...'

From an interview with Miwon Kwon in *Arte Joven en Nueva York,* Consejo Nacional de la Cultura, Caracas, 1991

Frankenstein in the Age of Biotechnology, 1991
Mixed media, variable dimensions
Installation at Gallery Christian Nagel, Cologne
Photo: Andrea Stappert

Mark Dion

Tropical Rainforest Preserves: Mobile Version, 1991
Mixed media, variable dimensions
Courtesy American Fine Arts, Co.

Mark Dion

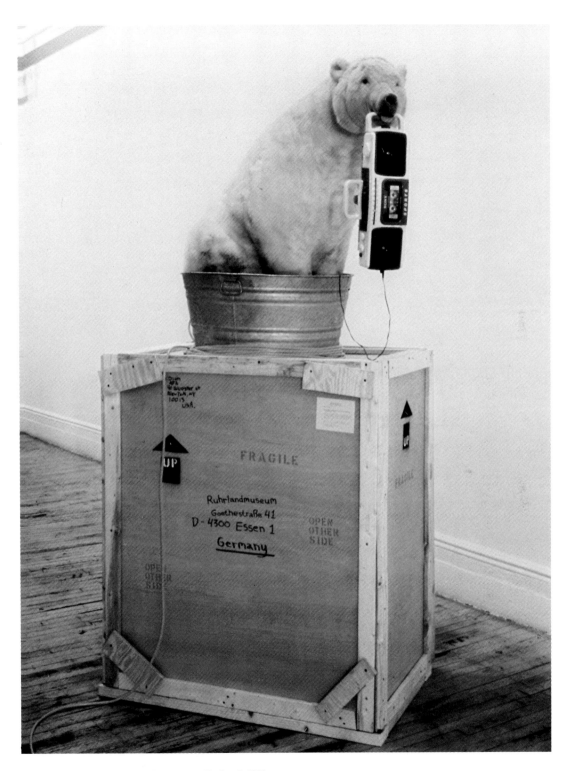

Polar Bears and Toucans (From Amazonas to Svalbard), 1991
Mixed media, 91" x 44" x 29¹/₂"
Courtesy American Fine Arts, Co.

Mark Dion

DAILY PLANET.

Science of the Planet

Frankenstein Abandons Creation

The Clark Kent Interviews:

Discussions in Science and Technology

Today: Dr. Victor Frankenstein
Visionary Microbiologist

Kent: Your presentation last week at the Hammer Conference on Biotechnology in London sparked an enormous controversy. In fact, it caused what can only be described as a riot. What did you say?

Frankenstein: I told the truth. The Hammer Conference is one of the few forums in which the popular press and the public directly interface with the bio-technocrats who control the genetic engineering industry. I merely presented a paper expressing concern over the direction the industry I helped to develop was going in, and answered some questions about ethics, safety and the scope of the biotechnology revolution.

I said that biotechnology leads us to reinvent ourselves to assume a more planetary role, that this entrancement allows us to recreate the natural world in our own image, to serve our needs of productivity and efficiency. What I did not do, is give the usual noble speech about the race to feed the planet and eliminate disease, because that is not necessarily what the companies which drive the bio-tech-revolution are interested in. Unless these pursuits translate into substantial profits.

Stating that this new technology was not a neutral tool in itself upset many people. Advanced science is something frightening to the public because it is a powerful and potentially destructive force with a history of abuse, because its goals and values are those of corporate or state leadership and because to many people, the idea of „progress" translates into something which endangers our lives and futures.

When a participant in the conference asked me why the public has so little say in the debate over biotechnology, I had to answer that it is because they have not challenged the shibboleth of progress. This is the ruling paradigm for science and technology. It dictates that once a technology is developed it will be used. What can be done must be done. The problem is that progress is essentially a matter of trial and error. Therefore, unlike my colleagues, I believe that the public's concern over the potential hazards of biotechnology arise not out of anti-intellectualism but out of legitimate concern. After all, commercialized genetics has proceeded with such haste – with little or no scrutiny or commentary from the outside – that the public re-

Kent: Can you explain to me what biotechnology is?

Frankenstein: When I say „biotech", I'm speaking narrowly, about genetic engineering. Over the past twenty years, researchers have made unprecedented developments in the direct manipulation of the genetic makeup of living things. This means the manipulation of genetic material through intervention at cellular and molecular levels rather than at the level of fully developed plants and animals. It is now possible to ship, insert, recombine, rearrange, edit, program and produce genetic material at the smallest possible scale –individual genes. This means that we can alter the very blueprint of life. We can give organisms traits from other organisms or we can produce novel organisms. At this point we are in the infancy of this technology. Genetic engineering is not so much a science yet, but rather a series of novel techniques, the effects of which are being investigated through the traditional scientific methods.

As a new technology, it promises many benefits and will have its most immediate impact on the commercial sectors of pharmaceuticals and agriculture. The products being developed fall into two broad categories: the chemical substances that can be synthesized from biologically engineered organisms (for

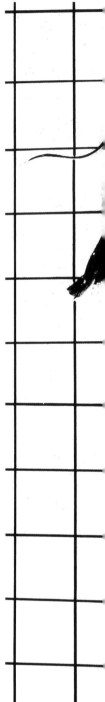

Photo: Jimmy Olsen

Dr. Frankenstein in the Age of Biotechnology

mains largely uninformed about its dimensions and implications.

What caused the most reaction was when I claimed that the official assurances of safety, in light of the past record of industrial mishaps.

in the chemical, nuclear and waste disposal industries, will no doubt prove false. This statement caused me to lose my positions on the advisory boards of both Monsanto and Hoechst.

example, hormones produced from engineered microbes) and genetically altered organisms themselves.

Kent: It does not seem, to me, that biotechnology is different from what breeders have been doing to improve agriculture for millennia.

Frankenstein: Selective breeding is to genetic engineering what the abacus is to the super computer. Make no mistake about this –

Continued on Page 2

Proposals On Genetic Technology

U.S. Panel Urges Easing of Regulation

By Edmund L.Andrews

Special from The New York Times

WASHINGTON, Feb.18 – A White House task force on biotechnology policy has recommended that the Government develop regulations that simplify the approval of genetically engineered crops, pesticides and animals.

In a report to be released Tuesday by the White House Council on Competitiveness, headed by Vice President Dan Quayle, the panel urges regulators to evaluate products made through gene splicing just as they would treat comparable products made through traditional methods.

If adopted by Government agencies, the recommendation could

A Genetically altered Catfish, grow bigger and faster than natural relatives.

Photo: Bob Braine

Continued on Page 2

break down sewage and toxic waste. But environmental groups, among others, warn of risks.

Seeks to Ignore Process

In essence, the report urges regulators to ignore the fact that such products are created through genetic engineering and to focus on a product's inherent characteristics. For example, regulators looking at a new breed of pest-resistant tomato would look at the plant's likelihood of becoming an out-of-control weed and at any risk posed by a toxin the plant may give off in fighting insects. The fact that the tomato was produced through ge-

New Prospects for Gene-Altered Fish Raise Hope and Alarm

WITH quickening speed, scientists are genetically engineering new strains of fish, producing faster-growing, larger strains but raising concerns about whether Government regulation will move fast enough to head off potential environmental problems.

„On one side of me I see people saying, 'Oh, my God! We're going to have Frankenstein fish.'" said Dr. Eric M. Hallerman, a geneticist at Virginia Polytechnic Institute and State University...On the other side I see people saying, 'We're going to feed the world.'"

Scientists have modified the genetic structure of goldfish, carp and channel catfish to make them grow bigger faster. Soon, they say, they will be able to create fish that withstand heat, cold, disease and toxins that pollute waterways, as well as sport and aquarium fish that are bigger, prettier and more feisty.

Though it will be some time before such fish appear on the nation's dinner tables, scientists say genetic engineering will transform commercial aquaculture, or fish farming.

Alarm Over Impact

In the five years since Chinese scientists first transferred a human growth hormone gene into goldfish, researchers have successfully transferred a foreign gene into fish at least 27 times. They have put genes from people, cattle, chickens, mice and other fish into a number of species from Atlantic salmon and rainbow trout to wall-

eye and northern pike.

The proliferation of experiments has alarmed environmentalists and many scientists, who say these new transgenic strains could profoundly disrupt fragile aquatic ecosystems.

„We have created new organisms," said David P. Philipp of the Illinois Natural History Survey, a state research center. „Without safeguards the release of these fish - whether intentional or inadvertent - has the potential of impact the environment."

Since the 1970's, when scientists learned how to isolate and splice genes, researchers have mixed genes from other species into scores of microbes, plants and mammals, including laboratory mice and farm animals such as cattle.

In 1985, researchers at the Institute of Hydrobiology at the Academy of Sciences in Wuhan, China, reported the first successful gene transfer in fish. The researchers, led by Dr. Zuoyan Zhu, injected a gene that regulates human growth into the eggs of 3,000 goldfish. As the eggs developed, the gene was integrated into the chromosomes of more than half the fish. Some of those grew to two or four times their normal size.

„It still needs some time, said Dr. Zhu, who is working at the Center for Marine Biotechnology at the University of Maryland. „But I think there is potential."

In many ways fish are proving easy to manipulate compared with mammals, since the female lays many large eggs that develop outside her body. Once scientists have isolated a gene they want to trans-

plant, they inject it into fish eggs using a microscopic needle. Then, by means they do not yet fully understand, the foreign gene is spliced into the chromosomes of some of the eggs.

Offspring Grew Faster

The first gene transfer in the United States was reported three years after Dr. Zhu's. Using a similar technique, a team of scientists from the University of Maryland, Johns Hopkins University and Auburn University transferred the gene that regulates growth in the rainbow trout into common carp.

The carp, which are kept in ponds on the Auburn campus in Alabama, have grown 20 to 40 percent larger than their natural relatives.

„Not only did they grow bigger and faster, but their offspring grew faster too." said Dr. Dennis A. Powers, a leader of the team.

Dr. Powers, now director of the Stanford University Hopkins Marine Station in Pacific Grove, Calif., and his colleagues, Dr. Thomas T. Chen at Maryland and Dr. Rex A. Dunham at Auburn, have also transferred the gene into channel catfish.

In Newfoundland, a research team has isolated the gene that allows the winter flounder to live in sub-zero temperatures through the winter and introduced it into Atlantic salmon.

The frigid waters of Newfoundland, where temperatures fall to about 28 degrees, are an inhospitable winter home for Atlantic

salmon, which cannot survive below about 30 degrees. Anti-freeze proteins in the winter flounder and other fish lower the freezing level of their blood.

Dr. Garth L. Fletcher of Memorial University of Newfoundland in St. John's said he has successfully integrated the gene that produces this protein into the salmon, though not yet at levels high enough to prevent the salmon's blood from freezing.

„It's a far-out experiment." said Eugene B. Henderson, director of the New Brunswick Salmon Growers Association. „But if in fact it worked, it would have a tremendous impact on the potential to grow salmon."

A 'Blue Revolution'

While it will be at least a few years before stable strains of genetically altered fish are ready for commercial use, scientists like Dr. Fletcher say their experiments will revolutionize fish farming, a $900 million industry in the United States.

Strains of fish that grow bigger faster and are resitant to diseases could spark a „blue revolution" in aquaculture in the way fertilizers, herbicides and pesticides sparked a „green revolution" in agriculture.

While the experiments have expanded scientists' understanding of genetics, many environmentalists and scientists say genetically altered fish could have an adverse impact on fragile aquatic ecosystems if ever released into the wild.

„Scientists ring up. 'Feed the world', and all objections are sup-

posed to fall away," said Dr. Jane F. Rissler of the National Wildlife Federation. „The question we have to ask is are the risks worth the benefits. Why are we exploiting the benefits of these organisms to satisfy our interests?"

For their part, scientists say they do not intend to release genetically altered fish into the wild but rather confine them to aquaculture farms or laboratory tanks.

Regulations Are Criticized

But environmentalists and scientists say that regulations in the United States controlling the research and release of genetically engineered fish are vague, allowing the opportunity for mistakes or abuse.

Since the early 1970's the National Institutes of Health in Bethesda, Md., has issued guidelines controlling recombinant DNA research in laboratories receiving Federal money and recommended that private institutions comply. The Department of Agriculture is in the process of setting its own guidelines over experiments conducted outdoors.

So far, only Dr. Zhu's fish in China and the carp and catfish in Alabama are being held outdoors, and in both cases the fish are confined in ponds covered in netting with drains wrapped in wire mesh to prevent escapes.

In the case of the Auburn carp, Dr. Rex Dunham requested permission from the National Institutes of Health and the Department of Agriculture to hold the fish in

outdoor ponds, though he said he was „technically and legally not required" to do so.

In Nov. 14, the Department of Agriculture approved a new request by Dr. Dunham to put into similar ponds hundreds of fry, the offspring of the roughly 50 transgenic carp and catfish in the ponds now.

Recognizing loopholes in regulations, the American Fisheries Society, an organization of fisheries scientists, has recommended that the Federal Government closely monitor experiments and tighten control over the release of altered fish into the environment.

In a report in a recent issue of its journal, Fisheries, the society recommended that genetically altered fish be sterilized before being released into the environment, perhaps by exposing them to chemicals in water while they are in the larval stage, whether in fish farms or in natural waterways.

Congressional efforts to impose regulations for the release of modified organisms have so far failed to gain momentum.

„Where it will eventually be decided is economics," said Perry B. Hackett Jr., a geneticist at the University of Minnesota, where scientists have genetically engineered rainbow trout, walleye and northern pike. „When the economics in the United States push for genetically altered fish, we're going to see genetically altered fish in one environment or another."

DO NOT FORGET THE NEEDIEST!

Concrete Jungle (The Birds), 1992
Mixed media, 110" x 102" x 102"
Installation at Tanja Grunert Gallery, Cologne

Mark Dion

The Department of Marine Identification of the City of New York (Chinatown Division), 1992
Marine animals collected in Chinatown, New York. Variable dimensions
Courtesy American Fine Arts, Co.
Photo: Angela Cumberbirch

Mark Dion

Renée Green

Essentially, Verne's explorers are name-givers;
they contribute to the world's genesis through
nomination. The leitmotif of the history: 'we gave
them the name Labyrinth because we had to make
several tries to find our way out'; the three islands
'received the name Baumann'; 'we call it Pitcairn';
'Bougainville could not refrain from giving it a new
name'; etc. The explorations semanticize the voids
of the universe. Their durations, accidents, episodes,
and trials metamorphose into words which fill the
indefinite expanses of the sea: 'the island of
Vexation', 'the Frigid Isles'. 'Arid Island', 'the island
of Appropriation', 'Betrayal Harbour', 'Desolation
Island' 'the Recreation Islands', etc. The voyages
write the Pacific's great white page: graphs of
journeys and words (fragments) from histories
traced on maps.

*Writing the Sea: Jules Verne, Heterologies,
Discourse on the Other*, Michel de Certeau, 1989,
University of Minnesota Press

"Friends", responded the engineer, "I think it would
be good to give this island a name, and also the
points, promontories and waterways we see before
our eyes."
"...In the future, it would simplify the instructions we
may have to give or follow."
"...Let us give them names like Robinson Crusoe's,
whose story Harbert has often read to me:
'Providence Bay,' 'Sperm Whale Promontory,'The
Cape of Vain Hope'!..."
"Or instead, "responded Harbert, "names like Smith,
Spilett, Nab!..."
"My name?" cried Nab, exhibiting his sparkling
white teeth.
"Why not?" replied Pencroft. "'Port Nab' would do
quite well! And 'Point Gedeon'..."

l'Iles Mysterieuse, Jules Verne

In order to be able to have an economy of travel,
some fixed point of reference must be posited. The
economy of travel requires an oikos (the Greek for
'home' from which is derived 'economy') in relation
to which any wandering can be comprehended
(enclosed as well as understood).

Travel as Metaphor: From Montaigne to Rousseau,
Georges Van Den Abbeele, 1992, University of
Minnesota Press

World Tour: Souvenirs (detail), 1992
Mixed media, Courtesy Pat Hearn Gallery, New York
Photo: Angela Cumberbirch

Case II (Lost), from *Anatomies of Escape*, 1990
ICA, The Clocktower Gallery, New York
Photo: Tom Warren

Renée Green

Sites of Genealogy, Loophole of Retreat, 1991 - 1992
PS1 Museum, Long Island City, NY
Photo: Tom Warren

Renée Green

Sites of Genealogy, Loophole of Retreat, 1991 - 1992
PS1 Museum, Long Island City, NY
Photo: Tom Warren

Renée Green

Bequest, 1991 - 1992
Installation view, Worcester Art Museum, Massachusetts

Overleaf - *World Tour: Souvenirs,* 1992
Mise en Scène (front), *Bequest,* (rear)
Mixed media, variable dimensions
Installation view, Pat Hearn Gallery, New York
Photo: Angela Cumberbirch

Renée Green

TRÉSOR
CACHÉ

POINT B

Import / Export Funk Office, 1992
Mixed media, installation view, Christian Nagel Gallery, Cologne
Photo: Andrea Stappert

Renée Green

Larry Johnson

Dear Editor:

Just a letter to "voice" my "concern" over what
can only be called "the unfortunate incident" that
took place at The Orange County Mensa's last
Halloween "party". Before we "close the door" on
this "unintended accident" I must ask that those
"responsible" for the "lamentable episode" explain,
from "beginning to end", ALL the "facts" of this so-
called "party" and "The Exploding Pumpkin Caper".
The lack of "judgement", even by a "non-mensa",
involved in putting a lit "cherry bomb" in a pumpkin
during the height of "The Fire Season" would be
deplorable. True, this is "An Orange Country Matter",
but the "harsh words" and "threats" "hurled" at those
"safety-minded" and "concerned" members of The
Los Angeles Mensa is a "truly vile" "turn" of "affairs."

L."B."J.
Los Angeles

Untitled (with Quotation Marks), 1992
Courtesy 303 Gallery, New York

Untitled, (A Quiet Life), 1991
Ektacolour photograph, 75" x 61"
Courtesy Jöhnen and Schöttle Gallery, Cologne and 303 Gallery, New York

Larry Johnson

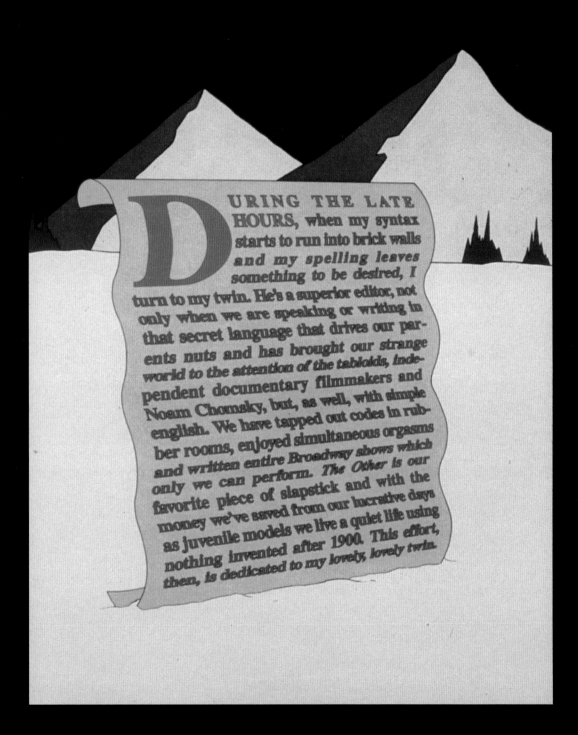

Untitled Negative, (A Quiet Life), 1991
Ektacolour photograph, 75" x 61"
Courtesy Jöhnen and Schöttle Gallery, Cologne and 303 Gallery, New York

Larry Johnson

THE YOUNG MAN wore black Hugo Boss and seemed happy to be here in Hollywood to have his story heard on T.V.'s HARD COPY. This homo hipster was no ordinary hophead hooligan, however. His hard-core habit and hard-fought holler for help hailed from the hallowed halls of higher learning: "When you do have a lot of students who are, whether they're maintaining the image, high profile, famous kids, children of presidents…That's just, you know, a tough environment."

Untitled Negative, (H), 1991
Ektacolour photograph, 57¹/₂" x 80"
Courtesy Jöhnen and Schöttle Gallery, Cologne and 303 Gallery, New York

Larry Johnson

THE RINGING! The non-stop and constant ringing! From the moment I arise, before my morning coffee: The ringing! From London and Paris they call, from Chicago and New York: promoters, directors, writers; my agents, my business and press people, my lawyers and my accountants. Would I do this? Could I do that? A television show, "Life With *Me*"? A radio program, "This Is *Me*"? A dramatic role on "*Me* She Wrote" or perhaps an "Afterschool *Me*"? Could I take my night-club act to Rio *Me* Janeiro? Maybe summer stock in *ME.*? *Me* Cosmetic Products? Or *Me* Fashion Creations? Would I appear as homecoming queen at Cal State *Me*? An Oscar? For *Me*? An award for being most fabulous? Most Glamorous? Most *Me*? Go on a coast-to-coast promotion for my thirteenth film, fly to Germany for my fourteenth, to England for my fifteenth? Hour after hour, offer after offer it goes; I have no time to stop and smell the rose named for *Me*.

Untitled Negative, (Winter Me), 1991
Ektacolour photograph, 57¹/₂" x 82"
Courtesy Jöhnen and Schöttle Gallery, Cologne and 303 Gallery, New York

Larry Johnson

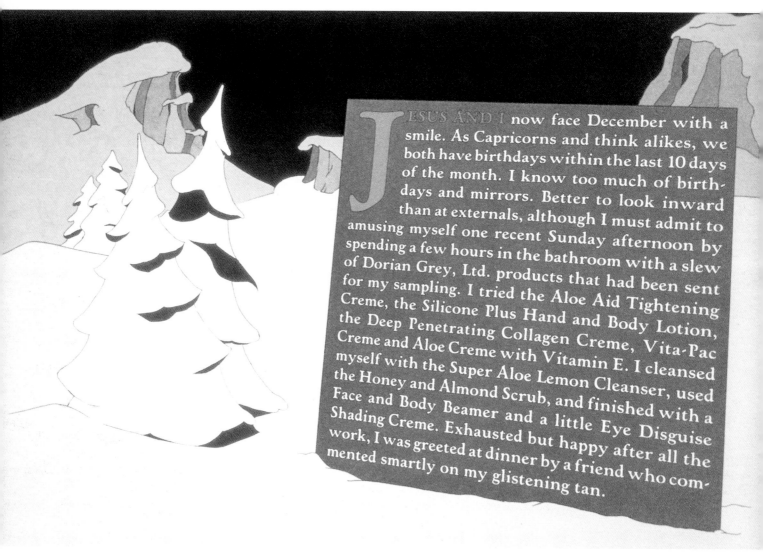

Untitled Negative, (Jesus and I), 1991
Ektacolour photograph, 57½" x 80"
Courtesy Jöhnen and Schöttle Gallery, Cologne and 303 Gallery, New York

Larry Johnson

Untitled Negative, (Dead and Buried), 1991
Ektacolour photograph, 57¹/₂" x 80"
Courtesy Jöhnen and Schöttle Gallery, Cologne and 303 Gallery, New York

Larry Johnson

Untitled Negative, (Classically Tragic Story), 1991
Ektacolour photograph, 57¹/₂" x 72"
Courtesy Jöhnen and Schöttle Gallery, Cologne and 303 Gallery, New York

Larry Johnson

Untitled Negative, (WXY + Z), 1991
Ektacolour photograph, 70" x 56"
Courtesy Jöhnen and Schöttle Gallery, Cologne and 303 Gallery, New York

Larry Johnson

Karen Kilimnik

A HARD DAY'S NIGHT, screenplay by Alun Owen; directed by Richard Lester and produced by Walter Shenson for United Artists. At the Astor, Broadway at 45th Street; the Trans-Lux East, Third Avenue at 58th Street, and other theaters in the metropolitan area. Running time: 87 minutes.

John	John Lennon
Paul	Paul McCartney
George	George Harrison
Ringo	Ringo Starr
Grandfather	Wilfrid Brambell
Norm	Norman Rossington
T V Director	Victor Spinelli
Shake	John Junkin
Millie	Anna Quayle
Simon	Kenneth Haigh
Man on Train	Richard Vernon
Hotel Waiter	Eddie Malin

By BOSLEY CROWTHER

THIS is going to surprise you—it may knock you right out of your chair—but the new film with those incredible chaps, the Beatles, is a whale of a comedy.

I wouldn't believe it either, if I hadn't seen it with my own astonished eyes, which have long since become accustomed to seeing disasters happen when newly fledged pop-singing sensations are hastily rushed to the screen. But this first fiction film of the Beatles, entitled "A Hard Day's Night," which exploded last night at the Astor, the Trans-Lux East and other theaters hereabouts, has so much good humor going for it that it is awfully hard to resist.

In the first place, it's a wonderfully lively and altogether good-natured spoof of the juvenile madness called "Beatlemania," the current spreading craze of otherwise healthy young people for the four British lads with the shaggy hair.

The opening shots, behind the credits, are of three of the fellows running ahead of a mob of howling admirers chasing after them as they break away from a theater where they have played a singing engagement and race for a waiting train. And all the way through the picture, there are frenzied episodes of the Beatles' encounters with squealing fans and with reporters who ask silly questions, all in a facile, witty vein.

But more than this, it's a fine conglomeration of madcap clowning in the old Marx Brothers' style, and it is done with such a dazzling use of camera that it tickles the intellect and electrifies the nerves.

This is the major distinction of this commercially sure-fire film: It is much more sophisticated in theme and technique than its seemingly frivolous matter promises. With practically nothing substantial in the way of a story to tell — nothing more than a loosely strung fable of how the boys take under their wings the wacky old grandfather of one of them while preparing for a London television show—it discovers a nifty little satire in the paradox of the old man being more of a problem, more of "a troublemaker and a mixer," than the boys.

"'e's a nice old man isn't 'e?," notes one of the fellows when they first meet Granddad on a train. And another replies, with courteous unction, which parodies the standard comment about the Beatles themselves, "'e's very clean."

This line, which runs through the picture, may be too subtle for the happily squealing kids who will no doubt be its major audience, but the oldsters may profitably dig. And, of course, everybody will be able to enjoy the rollicking, madcap fun.

There's no use in trying to chart it. It comes in fast-flowing spurts of sight gags and throw-away dialogue that is flipped about recklessly. Alun Owen, who wrote the screenplay, may have dug it all out of his brain, but Richard Lester has directed at such a brisk clip that it seems to come spontaneously.

And just one musical sequence, for instance, when the boys tumble wildly out of doors and race eccentrically about a patterned playground to the tune of their song "Can't Buy Me Love," hits a surrealistic tempo that approaches audio-visual poetry.

Sure, the frequent and brazen "yah-yah-yahing" of the fellows when they break into song may be grating. To

Wilfrid Brambell and Ringo Starr in scene from new movie

ears not tuned to it, it has moronic monotony. But it is always relieved by pictorial compositions that suggest travesties or, at least, intelligent awareness of the absurdity of the Beatle craze.

Unless you know the fellows, it is hard to identify them, except for Ringo Starr, the big-nosed one, who does a saucy comic sequence on his own. But they're all good

— surprisingly natural in the cinema-reality style that Mr. Lester expertly maintains. And Wilfrid Brambell as the old man is dandy, a delightfully comic Irishman. Many others are also funny.

It is good to know there are people in this world, up to and including the major parties, who don't take the Beatles seriously.

Ag 12, 1964, 41:1

THE PATSY, screenplay by Jerry Lewis and Bill Richmond, directed by Mr. Lewis and produced by Ernest D. Glucksman for Paramount. At neighborhood theaters. Running time: 101 minutes.

Stanley Belt	Jerry Lewis
Ellen Betz	Ina Balin
Caryl Fergusson	Everett Sloane
Chic Wymore	Phil Harris
Harry Silver	Keenan Wynn
Morgan Heywood	Peter Lorre
Bruce Alden	John Carradine
Professor Mulerr	Hans Conried

By BOSLEY CROWTHER

NOT having seen Jerry Lewis in the past three or four of his films—or since, in a rush of self-assurance, he took to directing himself—this reviewer, on seeing "The Patsy," his latest, was gratified to discover he's no better as a comedian than he used to be. The film opened at neighborhood theaters yesterday.

It would be in defiance of nature if Mr. Lewis improved. His idiot brand of clowning is granitic mediocrity. And for him to do anything for it by directing it himself would be as abhorrent to nature as all other vacuums are.

Thus it was reassuring to see that "The Patsy" is just another moronic mishmash in which Mr. Lewis falls all over himself. This time he is a clumsy bellboy in the Beverly Hilton Hotel who is picked for elevation to theatrical stardom by the writer-director-producer team of a famous comedian who has been killed in an accident. And the basis on which they pick him is that he looks so silly juggling a tray (which doesn't say much for the humor of their recent employer).

Anyhow, Mr. Lewis performs it by garbling and gulping his words, racing about in mad confusion, freezing up when he has to go on the stage and generally demonstrating his lack of coordination and wit. And sitting by, shaking their heads sadly as the injudicious production team, are Everett Sloane, Keenan Wynn, Peter Lorre, Phil Harris and John Carradine. Entirely in accord with their opinion of their Trilby is this reviewer.

Jerry Lewis

Also on the bill with "The Patsy" is "The Son of Captain Blood," an English-dubbed Italian swashbuckler starring Sean, the tall blond son of Errol Flynn. Let us just say that the old saw, "like father, like son," doesn't

DOCTOR, YOU'VE GOT TO BE KIDDING! screenplay by Phillip Shuken; directed by Peter Kewksbury; produced by Douglas Laurence for Metro-Goldwyn-Mayer. At neighborhood theaters. Running time: 94 minutes.

Heather Halloran	Sandra Dee
Harlan Wycliff	George Hamilton
Louise Halloran	Celeste Holm
Dick Bender	Bill Bixby
Pat Murad	Dick Kallman
Dan Ruskin	Mort Sahl
Hank	Dwayne Hickman
Joe Bonney	Allen Jenkins

SOMEBODY has got to be kidding about "Doctor, You've Got to Be Kidding!" Most likely, it's Metro-Goldwyn-Mayer. If the excruciating, tasteless little comedy that flapped into neighborhood theaters yesterday spells entertainment, then batten down the hatches.

Sandra Dee is loose again, folks. This go-round, the little blonde with the bee-stung lips and baby-fat cheeks sports some tight-fitting dresses to prove that even nice girls can drive the boys wild.

There's George Hamilton, for one, as her ice-cold executive boss who growls dictation until one day his eyes pop. Add a trio of hot-blooded chaps, smaller fry, hanging around her house at night, as her mama, Celeste Holm, tries to pound a show business career into Miss Dee with an anvil.

Miss Dee does get a kind of musical career going in a kind of night spot operated by a tired-looking Mort Sahl, who watches her doing a few wiggly gyrations, with a mewing diction that's supposed to be singing. "She's terrible," says Mr. Sahl, hiring her. Only about here, Mr. Hamilton having thawed considerably, Miss Dee finds she's pregnant. ("Doctor, You've Got To Be Kidding!"). And so forth and so on.

All this is supposed to be cute, breezy and friendly. "Mama," yelps Miss Dee, inspecting the family parakeet, "Reggie's laid an egg. "Honey, so has the picture.

HOWARD THOMPSON

My 11, 1967, 50:1

THE VISCOUNT, screenplay by Clark Reynolds, based on a novel by Jean Bruce; directed by Maurice Cloche; produced by Nat Wachsberger and presented by Warner Brothers. At neighborhood theaters. Running time: 98 minutes.

Clint de la Roche	Kerwin Mathews
Ricco Barone	Edmond O'Brien
Lili	Jane Fleming
Claudia	Yvette Lebon
Billette	Jean Yanne
Marco Demoyone	Fernando Rey
Tania	Maria Latour

and

THE COOL ONES, screenplay by Joyce Geller; adapted by Gene Nelson and Bob Kaufman from a story by Miss Geller; directed by Gene Nelson; produced by William Conrad and presented by Warner Brothers. At neighborhood theaters. Running time: 95 minutes.

Tony	Roddy McDowall
Hallie	Debbie Watson
Cliff	Gil Peterson
MacElwaine	Phil Harris
Stan	Robert Coote
Dee Dee	Nita Talbot
Howie	George Furch
Mrs. Miller	Mrs. Miller

By BOSLEY CROWTHER

"THE VISCOUNT," which gained admission to R.K.O. theaters yesterday, is an egregious impostor. It pretends to the title and the class of a high-born Bond-type picture and all it is is a low-grade gangster film—so low that it thinks Jersey City was the height of elegance as a center of crime in years gone by.

Charge that up to the fact that it is one of those European sausage films, ground out by a group of co-producers representing West Germany, France and Spain—and you know what usually happens when the Europeans try to show how wise they are about America.

Although it has Kerwin Mathews and Edmond O'Brien, both Hollywood emigrés, in its cast, the former playing the handsome hero and the latter a dope-ring boss, it is the sort of picture they'd be strongly inclined to brush under the rug in Hollywood—or quickly sell to television for burial on the late night shows.

It's full of fist fights, karate battles, automobile chases and machine-gun duels, and totally devoid of intelligence, humor, excitement or class.

On the bill with it is "The Cool Ones," a rock 'n' roll comedy, so-called, about a pop singer (Debbie Watson) who is on the rise and a big-name crooner (Gil Peterson) who is on the skids. Roddy McDowall is their manager who engineers them into a publicity romance which has—shall we say?—repercussions. I venture to guess this will disgust even the kids.

My 11, 1967, 50:1

You've Just Walked Into A TV Detective Show, 1989
Mixed media, variable dimensions
Courtesy 303 Gallery, New York

Karen Kilimnik

Hellfire Club of the Avengers, 1989
Mixed media, variable dimensions
Courtesy 303 Gallery, New York

Opposite - *Avengers with Roses,* 1991
Mixed media, variable dimensions
Courtesy 303 Gallery, New York

Karen Kilimnik

Mrs Peel... We're needed, 1992
Installation at Jennifer Flay Gallery, Paris
Mixed media, variable dimensions
Courtesy Jennifer Flay Gallery, Paris and 303 Gallery, New York

Karen Kilimnik

Battles or the Art of War, 1991
Mixed media, variable dimensions
Courtesy 303 Gallery, New York

Karen Kilimnik

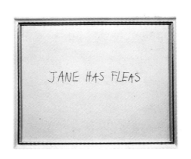

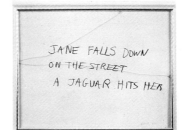

Jane Creep, 'Undertakers', 1991
Collection Mera and Donald Rubell

Jane Creep, 'Satan Worshippers', 1990
Collection Alice and Marvin Kosmin

Jane Creep, 'Dog Growl', 1990
Collection Anne Pasternak

Jane Creep, ' Hunting', 1990
Collection Ghisela Capitain

Jane Creep, 'Jaguar', 1989
Collection Richard Prince

Jane Creep, 'Pins in It', 1990
Collection Kay Heyman

Jane Creep, ' Magicians', 1990
Collection Andrew Renton

Jane Creep, 'Fleas', 1990
Collection Edward Merino

Jane Creep, 'Halloween Party', 1991
Collection Alice and Marvin Kosmin

All works, Crayon on paper, 11" x 14",
Courtesy 303 Gallery, New York

Karen Kilimnik

Brief Lives, 1990
Crayon on paper, 35" x 23"
Collection Liz and Kent Swig, courtesy 303 Gallery, New York

Karen Kilimnik

Raymond Pettibon

'And not that the real world was not enough to live on, but that the written version added so much more (as the written version of my life is so much different; so much better! one could almost say, having read it - the work in progress anyway) for all its abbreviation and omission; and the abridged version seemed all the righter (lighter still!) for what it left out, so that others might have the chance to spill their second-hand light on it for ink, and fill us in...

No wonder is it that God chose the written word to get it across, the good... Once brought down, next was to set it down, if not with His own implacable hand and its allover alignment of graven line... lest the world were made scrollwork that the word become flesh... but in His stead... His steadying hand, leading baton-like the dextral-textual transcription from high... from high-hat cymbal to orchestra pit snare... the word-by-word blow by-blow all-describable; or all that survives the translation (in decrescendo crashing down to earth)... or what's left of His signature to be allographed...

And to illustrate... (His work also)... the world

Amid the din of ambient dross that is our world in progress, a blank page of your own creation is a body of work more worthy than a library full of tomes, theses, and treatises; much erasing is involved here. To write 'The End' at the top of the page, and then erase that, is a picture worth countless thousands of words: not an illustration of the word, but the word's illuminations (white as the page it's written upon!), the word become parchment... The perfect manuscript: uncut, unopened, uninterpreted, unread: qualities that only the best of our literature can dare to lay claim to... And its cover black-on-Bible, containing every illuming color of monks working overtime, and every word of the text, set, laid in, printed; every line building on the preceding whole till every last smudge is crowded out, and there is not one undotted 'i' showing through... A picture for a story-book that tells all in one sight, for when one sees the cover, why ask of that which is hidden in?'

HOW IS THE AUTHOR TO WITH-
DRAW, TO STAND ASIDE, AND
TO LET THOUGHT TELL ITS
OWN STORY?

LOOKING OVER THE
AUTHOR'S SHOULDER:

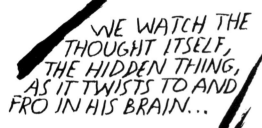

WE WATCH THE
THOUGHT ITSELF,
THE HIDDEN THING,
AS IT TWISTS TO AND
FRO IN HIS BRAIN...

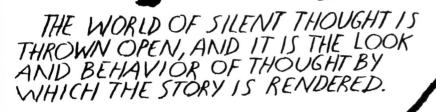

THE WORLD OF SILENT THOUGHT IS
THROWN OPEN, AND IT IS THE LOOK
AND BEHAVIOR OF THOUGHT BY
WHICH THE STORY IS RENDERED.

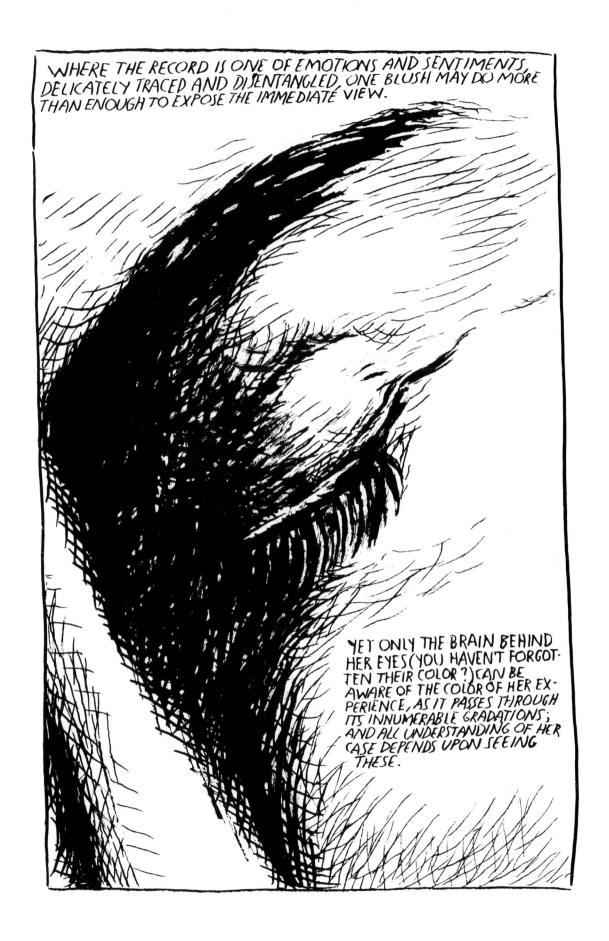

WHERE THE RECORD IS ONE OF EMOTIONS AND SENTIMENTS, DELICATELY TRACED AND DISENTANGLED, ONE BLUSH MAY DO MORE THAN ENOUGH TO EXPOSE THE IMMEDIATE VIEW.

YET ONLY THE BRAIN BEHIND HER EYES (YOU HAVEN'T FORGOTTEN THEIR COLOR?) CAN BE AWARE OF THE COLOR OF HER EXPERIENCE, AS IT PASSES THROUGH ITS INNUMERABLE GRADATIONS; AND ALL UNDERSTANDING OF HER CASE DEPENDS UPON SEEING THESE.

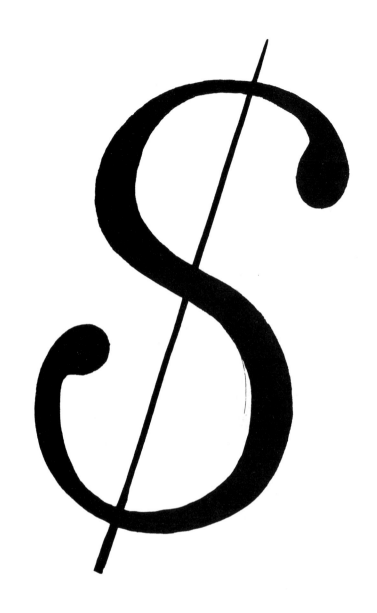

THE SKETCH IS AS COMPLETE AS IT IS RAPID,
AND A HOARY WORLD OF EXTORTION
AND OF STUPEFIED SUFFERANCE IS UN-
VEILED WITH A SINGLE GESTURE.

THAT IS THE VERY MIDDLE OF THE SUBJECT.

AND THAT IS SO FAR WELL ENOUGH,
AND PLAINLY NECESSARY.

AGAIN AND AGAIN
THE STROKE IS
ACCOMPLISHED, AND
THE AUTHOR GIVES HIM
ALMOST THE VALUE OF
AN INDEPENDENT PERSON.

THAT WHEN HE SPAT INTO
AN EYE THAT WAS BLIND OR
OBSCURE, THE SIGHT WAS AT
ONCE RESTORED TO IT.

THERE WAS A SHARP, ANGRY INTAKE OF BREATH AS SOMEBODY ON THE OTHER END GURGLED HIS LAST.

Jack Pierson

Kittens, as opposed to sensitive.

It was a really hot morning in Miami Beach, around the same time it is here now, but a few years ago. Andre was cutting my hair out on the third floor balcony that went around the courtyard of the 56 dollar-a-week hotel we were living in. Clayton was watching and doing his best to make me feel as though I were making a BIG mistake to risk Andre with my sun-fried hair. But I didn't care. Romeo the manager, who looked like an old Cuban running a well maintained flea bag hotel should look, came up the stairs and walked by us with that walk where his feet never seemed to leave the ground. Somehow letting us all know in a glance, a gesture, a word in Cuban that *he* should be cutting my hair, downstairs, in the courtyard, like he did the other men. It was all conveyed in this bemused way that let me know: no harm was done, next time, watch out for Andre and sweep the porch after. He had what I'd love, for the sake of this story to call a gunny sack, but I won't because it would be just too quaint. He was holding a burlap bag and he said something like "Ju es seen-es kitties" and he was holding open the door of the communal shower that no one ever uses. What? I thought. Then he went meow-meow and we all got what he meant and went down the other end to look. Kittens! The old dirty cat that was always around begging for food had a full litter of kittens in the shower stall. They were so cute as I'm sure you can imagine. Being all cute and sucking on that big old dirty mother Kitten. I wanted to get back to having my hair cut before Andre's train of thought pulled out of the station, forever. They'll be there for a while I thought and they're too little to pick up yet. So we went back to the not too short just a little trim business at hand. As we were finishing up, Romeo came back down the walk still carrying the burlap bag this time with something in it. Without thinking I asked What. meow-meow he sort of yawned and I got horrified for a minute, No Wait! I said, we'll keep em! No pets he said and pointed to a sign that would have been on the wall if we were down in the courtyard. Oh right, I said, trying to think. Miami Beach was over run with stray skinny old cats. Flagler had brought a million cats there in the Twenties and let em loose to try and solve the rat problem and they had been there growing in number ever since. What could I do? I got over it. I sat back down, sulking. He started back down the stairs I thought then and think now: How like *The Yearling* or the depression or the Thirties. How butch and like something my brothers would talk about doing to freak me out - then that joke of "Mommy, Mommy, Daddy took me swimming today and the mother says oh was it fun? Then the kid says yeah once I got out of the burlap sack." I tried to think Oh well I'm 25 now, that's life, I can handle it, who cares, a man's gotta do... Then I thought of Christine and Be Kind to Animals and the kittens in the sack under the water, drowning. But then I thought of them starving and skinny, running around the alley and I thought how kind and manly of Romeo, how... sensible.

Like so often back then and sometimes now I didn't know what to do so I just didn't do anything. I smoked a cigarette.

May 24th 1991 8:30am
Dedicated to Christine

A Fag, a Crip and a Chick

On following pages:
Tory
Vanessa
Rocky in Christine's Room
Rafael
Drive in Saturday
André and Clayton in an Empty Landscape

Jack Pierson

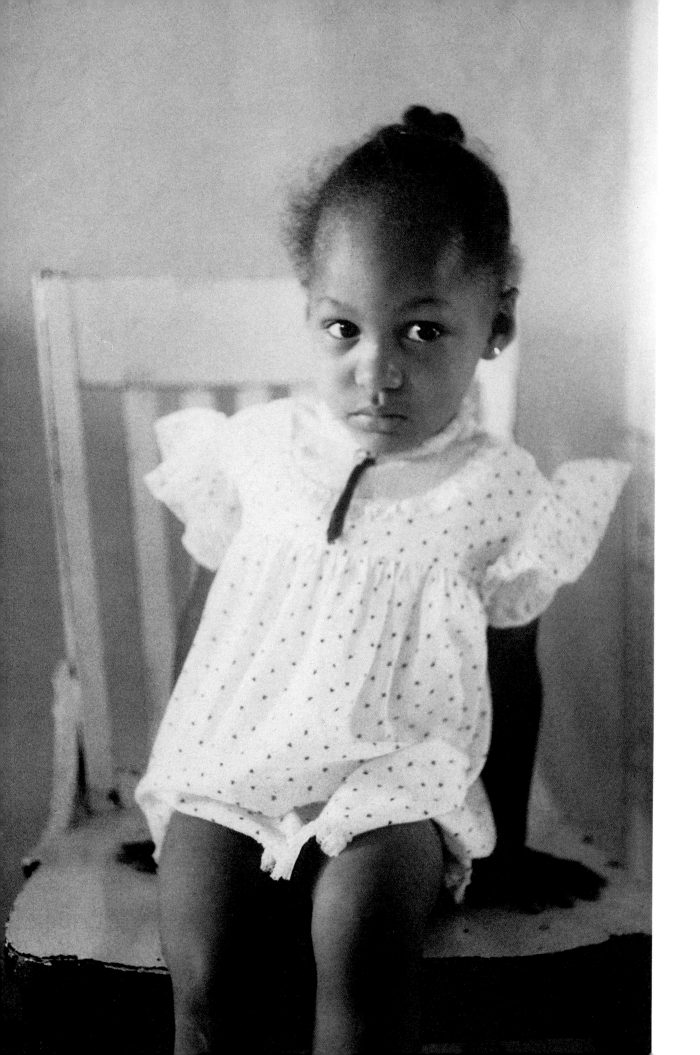

Jack Pierson

Jim Shaw

'*My Mirage* is a narrative in five chapters "written"
in one hundred and seventy plus pieces, set in 1960s
America, utilising as many aesthetics of the period
as could be crammed in. Billy, the protagonist, grows
up Christian, but the temptations of adolescence in
the secular, consumer world prove too much for him,
so he attempts to become innocent again through a
naive belief in psychedelia, having seen it in Time
magazine and on CBS. His new life involves
improvised rituals of passage (as the old ones have
ceased to have meaning for him), unrequited love
and a much bigger loss of innocence with a group of
"family" wanna-be's. In revulsion against his wild
teenage years he becomes a born again Christian
preaching against the sins and freedoms of his
experience in a final attempt to regain his innocence.

I have used texts, charts, comic books, narratives
and abstract paintings, videos and other art devices
to get the story across, albeit in a very cut up
method. The only kind of taste applied to the many
aesthetics involved is the 17" x 14" format.
By shrinking occasional high cultural elements in
scale and using adolescent materials such as model
parts and modelling clay, I have tried to deflate
some conceits and see what holds up on a reduced
scale (down from heroic), which is the scale I
experienced art as an adolescent, in reproductions
in my small town library. I made a motif of ordering
and systematizing (which is Billy's only way of
dealing with an unkempt and morally ambiguous
world) and without intending to, my own aesthetic
of obsessiveness and fear comes through. I have
tried not to shy away from the direct, although
repeated viewing will hopefully reveal a ridiculous
complexity of symbolism and cross referencing.
What is on view in this exhibit is a slice of the whole;
some elements will be missing, while others will
be in the American vernacular, but I hope enough
content comes through to make some sense of
the whole.'

Opposite - *My Mirage Logo No. 3,* 1989
Silkscreen on paper, 17" x 14", edition 18 / 30
Linda Cathcart Gallery, Santa Monica

Post 1988
Acrylic on board, 17" x 14"
Courtesy Linda Cathcart Gallery, Santa Monica

Jim Shaw

Debemus, 1990
Oil on canvas, 17" x 14"
Collection Flora Biddle

Esse, 1990
Oil on canvas, 17" x 14"
Collection Edward R. Downe Jr.

Jim Shaw

Mortui, 1990
Oil on canvas, 17" x 14"
Courtesy Linda Cathcart Gallery, Santa Monica

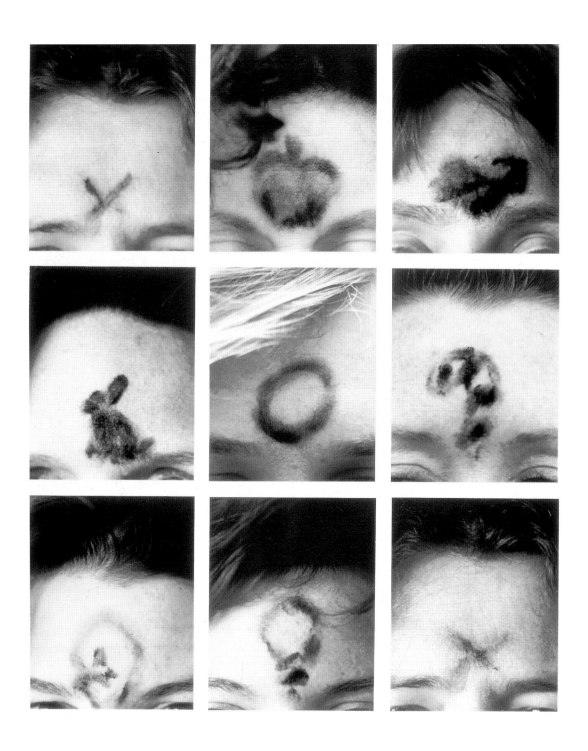

Charcoal Drawing, 1990
Cibachrome print, 17" x 14"
Collection Barry Sloane, Los Angeles

Jim Shaw

Icon (Pizza Face), 1990
Gouache on board, 17" x 14"
Collection Barry Sloane, Los Angeles

Jim Shaw

Chicago 68, 1991
Gouache on board, 17" x 14"
Collection Linda and Jerry Janger, Los Angeles

Opposite - *Untitled (Teenagers Talking),* 1991
Ink on board, 17" x 14"
Collection Arthur and Carol Goldberg, New York

Jim Shaw

Mark Dion

Biography

1961 Born New Bedford, Massachusetts
1992 Lives New York

Selected Exhibitions

1985 Four Walls, Hoboken, New Jersey
1986 *Rooted Rhetoric*, Lia Rumma Gallery, Naples
Cutting 'Em Off at the Pass, Atlanta Arts Festival, Atlanta
The Fairy Tale; Politics, Desire and Everyday Life, Artists Space, New York
1987 *Fake!*, The New Museum of Contemporary Art, New York
The Castle, Group Material Exhibit at Documenta, Kassel
303 Gallery, New York
1988 *The Pop Project Part IV. Nostalgia as Resistance*, The Clocktower, New York
Artists and Curators, John Gibson Gallery, New York
1989 *Perspektivismus*, Graz, Austria
The Desire of the Museum, Whitney Museum of American Art, New York
Artful History: A Restoration Comedy, Collective for Living Cinema, New York
American Fine Arts Co., New York
1990 Mark Dion with William Schefferine, American Fine Arts Co., New York
The (Un)Making of Nature, Whitney Museum of American Art, New York
Extinction. Dinosaurs and Disney, Galerie Sylvana Lorenz, Paris
Biodiversity, Wexner Center for Visual Arts, Ohio
Commitment, The Power Plant, Toronto
1991 *Frankenstein in the Age of Biotechnology*, Christian Nagel Galerie, Cologne
True to Life, 303 Gallery, New York
Arte Joven en Nueva York, Sala Mendoza, Consejo Nacional de la Cultura, Caracas, Venezuela
Art...not News, Real Art Ways, Hartford, Connecticut
1992 American Fine Arts, Co., New York
Tanja Grunert Galerie, Cologne

Selected Bibliography by the Artist

1988 'Tales from the Darkside', *Real Life Magazine*, no. 14
1989 'Terra Ferma', *The Silent Baroque*, catalogue, Galerie Thaddaeus Ropac, Salzburg
Polar Bears and Toucans, catalogue, Le Magasin, Grenoble
1991 'Die Botschaft als Medium', *Der Standard*, project for museum in progress, Vienna, January
'Frankenstein Abandons Creation', *Daily Planet-Science of the Planet*, Cologne, 5th April
Dion, Mark and Rockman, Alexis, 'Concrete Jungle', *Journal of Contemporary Art*, vol. 4 no. 1, Spring / Summer

Selected Bibliography

1987 Indiana, Gary, 'Agitation', *The Village Voice*, 28th July
1988 Lawson, Thomas, 'Nostalgia as Resistance', *Modern Dreams: The Rise and Fall and Rise of Pop*, The MIT Press, pp. 170-171
Cembalest, Robin, 'Restoration Tragedies', *Art News*, May
Weaver, Frank, review, *Flash Art*, no. 149, November / December
1990 Decter, Joshua, 'New York in Review', *Arts Magazine*, Summer, p. 97
Matola, Sharon, 'Belize Zoo: Construction / Conservation Update', *On the Edge*, Wildlife Preservation Trust Int'l, Summer, p. 12
Lewis, James, review, *Artforum*, September, p. 154
Zimmer, William, 'Conceptual Works Issue Dire Warnings', *The New York Times*, 28th October
Reproduction, *Beaux Arts - Special USA*, October, p. 33
Graw, Isabelle, 'Field Work', *Flash Art*, November / December, pp.136-137
Decter, Joshua, 'Decoding the Museum', *Flash Art*, November / December, pp. 140-42
Praet, Michel van, 'Renovating Nature', *Flash Art*, no. 155, November / December, pp. 132-133
1991 Avgikos, Jan, 'Green Peace', *Artforum*, April, pp. 104-110
Diederichsen, Diedrich and Koether, Jutta, 'Die Nagel trifft den Kopf', *Spex*, April
Vogel, Sabine B., 'Verortungen Installation', *Arts*, June, pp. 40-45
1992 Smolik, Noemi, review, *Artforum*, Summer

Renée Green

Biography
1959 Born Cleveland, Ohio
1992 Lives New York

Solo Exhibitions
1988 Jersey City Museum, New Jersey
1990 *Anatomies of Escape*, The ICA, The Clocktower,
     New York Harlem School of the Arts, New York
1991 Pat Hearn Gallery, New York
     The Worcester Art Museum, Massachusetts
1992 *Import / Export Funk Office*, Galerie Christian Nagel,
     Cologne
     Pat Hearn Gallery, New York

Selected Group Exhibitions
1989 *From the Studio: Artists in Residence*, 1988-89,
     The Studio Museum in Harlem, New York
1990 *Selections Aljira and Artists Space*, Artists Space,
     New York
     Social Studies: 4 + 4 Young Americans, Allen Memorial
     Art Museum, Oberlin College, Ohio
     Nicole Klagsbrun Gallery, New York
     Out of Site, P.S. 1 Museum / Institute of Contemporary
     Art, Long Island
     The Construction of Knowledge, Diane Brown Gallery,
     New York, Nicole Klagsbrun Gallery, New York
1991 *SiteSeeing: Travel and Tourism in Contemporary Art*,
     Whitney Museum of American Art, New York
     New Generations: New York, Carnegie Mellon Art
     Gallery, Pittsburg
     Natural History, Barbara Farber Gallery, Amsterdam
     Arte Joven en Nueva York, Sala Mendoza, Consejo
     Nacional de la Cultura, Caracas, Venezuela
     Lost Illusions: Recent Landscape Art, Vancouver Art
     Gallery, Canada
1992 *Dirty Data*, Sammlung Schurmann 1992, Ludwig Forum
     for International Art, Aachen
     Multiple Cultures, Convent of San Egidio, Rome
     Inheritance, LACE, Los Angeles
     Mary Kelly / Renée Green, Herbert F. Johnson Museum
     of Art, Cornell University, Ithica, New York
     Speak, Randolph Street Gallery, Chicago
     Huitiemes Ateliers Internationaux Pays de Loire,
     F.R.A.C., Clisson, France

Selected Publications by the Artist
1981 *No Title - The Collection of Sol Le Witt*, ed. John Paoletti,
     Wesleyan University/Wadsworth Atheneum, Hartford,
     Conneticut
1990 'I Won't Play Other to Your Same', *Meaning 7*, May,
     pp. 15-16
     What's Painting Got To Do With It?: Art in the Age of
     Post Mechanical Production, *Post-Boys and Girls: Nine
     Painters*, Artists Space, New York, pp. 8-10
1991 'Trading on the Margin', *Transition: An International
     Review*, no. 52, pp. 124-32
     'Democracy in Question', *Transition: An International
     Review*, no. 53, pp. 163-167

'Sites Of Geneology' and 'I Won't Play Other to Your
Same', *Text zur Kunst*, Summer
'Cold Sweat', *Texte zur Kunst*, Fall
1992 'Der Offentliche Blick', Artists Pages, *Jahresring*, no. 38
     'Black Popular Culture?' *Texte zur Kunst*, Winter, and
     Art and Text, Summer

Selected Bibliography
1989 Brenson, Michael, 'Show at the Studio Museum of its
     Artists in Residence', *The New York Times*,
     15th December
1990 Brenson, Michael, 'Renée Green - Anatomies of
     Escape', *The New York Times*, 25th May
     Bishop, Kathy, 'Fanfare', *Vanity Fair*, June
     Levin, Kim, 'Turning the Tables' and 'Choices',
     The Village Voice, I9th June
     Brown, Elizabeth, *Social Studies: 4 + 4 Young
     Americans*, catalogue, Alan Memorial Art Museum,
     Oberlin College, Bulletin 44, no.1
     Brendan, Gill, 'Manhattan's Arena for Aesthetic
     Melodrama', *Architectural Digest*, no. 47, November
1991 Oleksijczuk, Denise, *Lost Illusions: Recent Landscape
     Art*, catalogue, Vancouver Art Gallery
     Kontova, Helena, 'Interview: Robert Nickas', *Flash Art*,
     January / February
     Foster, Hal, 'Convulsive Identity', *October* no. 57,
     Summer
     Denson, Roger G., 'A Genealogy of Desire: Renée
     Green Explores the Continent of Power', *Flash Art*,
     no. 24, October
     Harkavy, Donna, *Renée Green, 'Bequest'*, catalogue,
     Worcester Art Museum, Massachusetts
     Nickas, Robert, *Natural History*, catalogue, Barbara
     Farber Gallery, Amsterdam
     King, Elaine, *New Generations: New York*, catalogue,
     Carnegie Mellon Art Gallery, Pittsburgh
     Higa, Karin, *SiteSeeing: Travel and Tourism in
     Contemporary Art*, catalogue, Whitney Museum of
     Contemporary Art, New York
1992 Cameron, Dan, 'Critical Edge', *Arts*, January
     Smith, Roberta, 'Renée Green: Pat Hearn Gallery', *The
     New York Times*, 1st May
     Agvikos, Jan, 'Renée Green: Pat Hearn Gallery',
     Artforum, Summer
     Zahm, Olivier, 'Mise en Scene', *Huitiemes Ateliers
     Internationaux des Pays dè la Loire*, F.R.A.C.,
     catalogue, Clisson, France and 'Nantes und die
     Geschichte des Sklavenhandels', *Texte zur Kunst*, no. 5,
     Winter
     Nieswandt, Hans, 'Green ist die Hoffnung', *Spex*, August
     Obrist, Hans Ulrich, 'The Installation is Coming Through
     the Back Door', *Meta 1- Die Kunst und ihr ort*,
     Kunstlerhaus, Stuttgart
     Schurmann, Wilhelm, *Dirty Data*, catalogue, Ludwig
     Forum for International Art, Aachen
     Mercer, Kobena, Decter, Joshua, *Inheritance*,
     catalogue, LACE, Los Angeles

Larry Johnson

Biography
1959   Born Long Beach, California
1992   Lives Los Angeles, California

Solo Exhibitions
1986   303 Gallery, New York
1987   303 Gallery, New York
      Kuhlenschmidt / Simon Gallery, Los Angeles
      Galerie Isabella Kacprzak, Stuttgart
1989   303 Gallery, New York
      Le Case d'Arte, Milan
1990   Stuart Regen Gallery, Los Angeles
      303 Gallery, New York
      Galerie Isabella Kacprzak, Cologne
1991   303 Gallery, New York
      Johnen and Schottle, Cologne
      Rena Bransten Gallery, San Francisco

Selected Group Exhibitions
1984   *Three Artists Select Three Artists*, Artists Space,
      New York
1985   *James Casebere, Larry Johnson, Jeff Koons*,
      303 Gallery, New York
1987   *The Castle*, installation by Group Material at
      Documenta 8, Kassel
      Larry Johnson, Tony Tassett, Christopher Wool,
      Kuhlenschmidt / Simon Gallery, Los Angeles
      CalArts - Skeptical Belief(s), The Renaissance Society at
      The University of Chicago, Chicago and Newport
      Harbor Art Museum, Newport Beach, California
      Contemporary Diptych: Divided Vision, Whitney
      Museum of American Art, Stamford, Connecticut and
      Equitable Center, New York
1988   *Utopia Post Utopia*, ICA, Boston
      Aperto '88', Venice Biennale XLIII, Venice
      Larry Johnson, Liz Larner, Charles Ray, 303 Gallery,
      New York
      Modes of Address: 25 Years of Language in Art,
      Whitney Museum of American Art, New York
1989   *A Forest of Signs*, Museum of Contemporary Art,
      Los Angeles
      California Photography: Remaking Make-Believe,
      Museum of Modern Art, New York and tour
      The Photography of Invention, National Museum of
      Art, Smithsonian Institution, Washington and Museum
      of Contemporary Art, Chicago
      Image World, Whitney Museum of American Art,
      New York
      Art About Aids, Freedman Gallery, Albright College,
      Reading, PA
1990   *Word as Image: American Art 1960-1990*, Milwaukee
      Art Museum, Milwaukee and tour
      De Afstandt, Witte De With, Centre for Contemporary
      Art, Rotterdam
      Charade of Mastery, Whitney Museum of
      Contemporary Art, New York
      Language in Art, The Aldrich Museum of
      Contemporary Art, Ridgefield, Connecticut

1991   *Words and Numbers*, Museum of Contemporary Art,
      Wright State University, Dayton, Ohio
      Whitney Biennale, New York
      *A Dialogue About Recent American and European
      Photography*, Museum of Contemporary Art,
      Los Angeles
      Aussenraum-Innenstadt, Sprengel Museum, Hannover

Selected Bibliography
1987   Whitney Museum of American Art, New York
      Cal Arts: Skeptical Belief(s), catalogue , The
      Renaissance Society at The University of Chicago and
      The Newport Harbor Art Museum
1988   *Modes of Address: Language in Art Since 1960*,
      Whitney Museum of American Art, New York
1989   Heiferman, Philips and Hanhardt, *Image World*,
      catalogue, Whitney Museum of American Art, New York
1990   *Word as Image*, catalogue, Milwaukee Art Museum,
      p. 117
      *The Charade of Mastery: Deciphering Modernism in
      Contemporary Art*, catalogue, Whitney Museum of
      American Art, New York
      Grundberg, Andy, 'Hybrids by Larry Johnson that
      Stretch Language to Its Limits', *The New York Times*,
      March 30, p. 22
      Rimanelli, David, interview, *Flash Art*, vol. XXIII no. 155,
      November / December, pp. 121-123
      Knight, Christopher, review, 'The Rime and Reason of
      Stories Coldly Told', *The Los Angeles Times*, 20th
      December, p. 16
1991   Myers, Terry, 'Hard Copy, the Sincerely Fraudulent
      Photographs of Larry Johnson', *Arts Magazine*,
      Summer, pp. 40-45

Karen Kilimnik

Biography
1962   Born Philadelphia
1992   Lives Brooklyn

Selected Solo Exhibitions
1991   303 Gallery, New York
1992   *Karen Kilimnik: Escape in Time*, ICA, Philadelphia
      Galerie Jennifer Flay, Paris
      Galerie Esther Schipper, Cologne
      Galerie Gisela Capitain, Cologne

Selected Group Exhibitions
1988   Cable Gallery, New York
1989   American Fine Arts Co., New York
      Nicole Klagsbrun Gallery, New York
1990   *Work in Progress? Work?*, Andrea Rosen Gallery,
      New York
1991   *Karen Kilimnik, Raymond Pettibon, and Allen Ruppersberg*,
      303 Gallery, New York
      No Man's Time, Villa Arson, Nice
      When Objects Dream And Talk in Their Sleep,
      Jack Tilton Gallery, New York
      Karen Kilimnik, Liz Larner, Collier Schorr, Anne Walsh,
      Richard Kuhlenschmidt Gallery, Santa Monica
      Just What is it That Makes Today's Homes So Different,
      So Appealing?, The Hyde Collection, Glens Falls, New York
      Plastic Fantastic Lover (object a), Blum Helman
      Warehouse, New York
      Residue Politics, Beaver College Art Gallery, Glenside,
      Philadelphia
1992   *Post-Human*, FAE Musee D'Art Contemporain, Lausanne
      Tatoo Collection, Air de Paris, Paris
      Lifesize, Museo D'Arte Contemporanea, Prato
      Are you a Boy, Or Are You A Girl? Real Art Ways,
      Hartford, Connecticut

Selected Bibliography
1990   Akvigos, Jan, 'Disappearing Acts', *Contemporanea*,
      no. 23, p. 72-75
      'Project', *Bomb*, Spring, pp.48-49
      Smith, Roberta, 'Critics Choice': Karen Kilimnik
      The New York Times, Fri. April 26th, p.17
1991   Bankowsky, Jack, 'Openings: Karen Kilimnik',
      Artforum, May, p. 138
      Saltz, Jerry, 'The Kid Who Never Cleaned Her Room',
      Galleries Magazine, July, p. 80-81
      Bankowsky, Jack, 'Slackers', *Artforum*, November,
      pp. 96-100
      Troncy, Eric, 'No Man's Time', *Flash Art*, November/
      December, pp. 119-122
1992   Feldman, Melissa, *Karen Kilimnik: Escape in Time*,
      catalogue, ICA, Philadelphia
      Benjamin, Weil, 'Remarks on Installations and
      Changes in Time Dimensions', *Flash Art*, March/
      April, pp. 104-109
      Bourriaud, Nicolas, 'Psycho-Splatter', *Flash Art*,
      March/ April, pp. 89-90

Raymond Pettibon

Biography

Selected Solo Exhibitions

Selected Group Exhibitions

Selected Bibliography

1989 Decter, Joshua, 'New York in Review', *Arts*, Summer,
      p. 93

1990 Rugoff, Ralph, *Just Pathetic*, catalogue, Rosamund
      Felsen Gallery, Los Angeles
      Weissman, Benjamin, review, *Artforum*, May, p.197

1991 Bernard, Bourriaud, Jouannais, Troncy, *No Man's Time*,
      Villa Arson catalogue, Nice
      Myles, Eileen, review, *Art in America*, March,
      pp. 141-142
      Koether, Jutta, 'Billy, Mike, Jim and Ray', *Kölner
      Illustrierte*, July, p. 8
      Hixson, Kathryn, 'News Reviews', *Flash Art*,
      October, p. 72
      Myers, Terry R., review, *Art Issues*, November/
      December, pp. 30-31

      Troncy, Eric, 'No Man's Time', *Flash Art*, November/
      December, pp.119-122

1992 Schimmel, Klein, Relyea, *Helter Skelter: L.A. Art in
      the 1990s*, Museum of Contemporary Art catalogue,
      Los Angeles
      Knight, Christopher, 'An Art of Darkness at MOCA',
      The Los Angeles Times, 28th January, p. F1, F4-6
      Plochere, Michelle, 'A Conversation with Raymond
      Pettibon', *Artweek*, 6th Febuary, p. 20
      Gerstler, Amy, review, *Artforum*, March, pp. 114-115
      Metzger, Rainer, review, *Flash Art*, March / April, p. 121
      Anderson, Michael, review, *Art Issues*, March / April,
      p. 39
      Zellen, Jody, 'Raymond Pettibon', review, *Arts*, April,
      p. 80
      Rugoff, Ralph, 'Spotlight', *Flash Art*, May / June, p. 108

Jack Pierson

Biography
1960 Born Plymouth, Massachusetts
1992 Lives New York

Solo Exhibitions
1990 Simon Watson, New York
1991 Pat Hearn Gallery, New York
Richard Kuhlenschmidt Gallery, Santa Monica
1992 Tom Cugliani Gallery, New York
White Columns, New York
Aurel Scheibler, Cologne

Group Exhibitions
1990 *Blood Remembering*, Snug Harbour Art Center,
Staten Island, New York
eros / thanatos death and desire, Tom Cugliani Gallery,
New York
1991 *Selections 51*, The Drawing Center, New York
Phillip Lorca Di Corcia, Nan Goldin and Jack Pierson,
York University, Toronto
From Desire..., Richard F. Brush Gallery,
St.Lawrence University, Canton, New York
Something Pithier and more Psychological, Simon
Watson, New York
Someone or Somebody, Meyers/Bloom Gallery,
Santa Monica
Drawings, Lorence-Monk, New York
Situations, New Langton Arts, San Francisco
Presenting Rearwards, Rosamund Felsen Gallery,
Los Angeles
Aurel Scheibler, Cologne
Andrea Rosen Gallery, New York
1992 *How It Is*, Tony Shafrazi Gallery, New York
Jack Hanley Gallery, San Francisco
Healing, Wooster Gardens, New York
Drawings, Stuart Regen Gallery, Los Angeles
Pat Hearn Gallery, New York

Selected Bibliography
1991 Schwartzman, Alan, 'Goings on about Town', *The New
Yorker*, 25th March
Saltz, Jerry, 'Shelter from the Storm', *Arts*, September
Bankowsky, Jack, 'Slackers', *Artforum*, November
Avgikos, Jan, 'Openings: Jack Pierson', *Artforum*,
December
1992 Connelly, John, review, *Flash Art*, March/April
Denton, Monroe, review, *Teme Céleste*, April/May

Jim Shaw

Biography
1952 Born Midland, Michigan
1992 Lives Los Angeles, California

Selected Solo Exhibitions
1990 Linda Cathcart Gallery, Santa Monica
Jim Shaw: My Mirage, catalogue, Matrix Gallery,
University Art Museum, University of California at
Berkeley and St. Louis Museum of Art, Missouri
Feature Gallery, New York
1991 *New Works from 'My Mirage'*, Linda Cathcart Gallery,
Santa Monica
1992 *Horror A Vacui*, Linda Cathcart Gallery, Santa Monica

Selected Group Exhibitions
1987 *L.A.: Hot and Cool; The Eighties*, catalogue, MIT List
Visual Arts Center, Cambridge, Massachusetts
Cal Arts; Skeptical Belief(s), The Renaissance Society
at the University of Chicago, Illinois and Newport Harbor
Art Museum, Newport Beach, California
1988 *Telling Tales*, Artists Space, New York
1989 *Erotophobia*, Simon Watson Gallery, New York
Amerikarma, Hallwalls, Buffalo
1990 *Recent Drawings: Roni Horn, Charles Ray, Jim Shaw,
Michael Tetherow*, catalogue, Whitney Museum of
American Art, New York
Berlin Film and Video Festival
1991 *No Man's Time*, Villa Arson, Nice
Whitney Biennial, catalogue, Whitney Museum of
American Art, New York
1992 *Helter Skelter; L.A. Art in the 1990s*, catalogue, Museum
of Contemporary Art, Los Angeles
*Group Show: Ronald Jones, Robert Longo, Mike Kelly,
Jim Shaw*, Metro Pictures, New York
How it is, Tony Shafrazi Gallery, New York
Just Pathetic, American Fine Arts Co., New York

Selected Bibliography
1990 Saltz, Jerry, 'Lost in Translation: Jim Shaw's
Frontispieces', *Arts Magazine*, vol. 64 no. 10, Summer
Knight, Christopher, 'Shaw's Wildly Funny Narrative
Saga', *Los Angeles Times*, 7th December, p. 19
1991 Larson, Kay, 'A Shock To The System', *New York*, 20th
April, vol. 24 no. 17, pp. 86-7
Knight, Christopher, 'Four Floors of Evolution', *Los
Angeles Times*, Calendar Section, 28th April, p. 3
Kimmelman, Michael, 'At The Whitney, A Biennial
That's Eager To Please', *The New York Times*, 19th April
Lois E. Nesbitt, 'American Psycho', *Artscribe*, September,
pp. 42-47
Troncy, Eric, 'No Man's Time', *Flash Art*, November/
December, pp. 121-122
1992 Rugoff, Ralph, 'Recycling the Subcultural Straightjacket',
Flash Art, March/April, pp. 91-3

True Stories

Part 1: Larry Johnson, Karen Kilimnik,
Jack Pierson, Raymond Pettibon, Jim Shaw
16 September - 25 October 1992

Part 2: Mark Dion, Renée Green
4 November - 6 December 1992

© The Artists, Iwona Blazwick, Emma Dexter, ICA

The Institute of Contemporary Arts is an
independent educational charity and while
gratefully acknowledging the financial assistance
of the Arts Council of Great Britain, Westminster
City Council, the British Film Institute and the
Rayne Foundation, is primarily reliant on its box
office income, membership and donations.

ICA Director: *Mik Flood*
Exhibition Curators: *Iwona Blazwick* and
Emma Dexter
Exhibition Coordinator: *Ingrid Swenson*
Administrator: *Gillian Adam*
Gallery Manager: *Angus Howie*
Publications Coordinator: *Ragnar Farr*
Exhibition Intern: *Jemima Rellie*

ICA, The Mall, London SW1Y 5AH
Telephone: 071 930 3647

Design by *Form*, London
Cover photograph by *Trevor Ray Hart*
Printed by *Lecturis*, Eindhoven

ISBN 0 905263 78 2